The Trial of Dr John Bodkin Adams

by David Holding

First published by
Scott Martin Productions, 2020
www.scottmartinproductions.com

First published in Great Britain in 2019 by
Scott Martin Productions
10 Chester Place,
Adlington, Chorley, PR6 9RP
lesley@scottmartinproductions.com
www.scottmartinproductions.com

Electronic version and paperback versions available for purchase on Amazon.
Copyright (c) David Holding and Scott Martin Productions.

First edition 2020.

The right of David Holding to be identified as the author of this work has been asserted by him in accordance with the Copyright, Design and Patents Act 1988.

All rights reserved. Without limiting the rights under copyright reserved above, no part of this publication may be reproduced, stored or introduced into a retrieval system, or transmitted, in any form or by any means (electronic, mechanical, photocopying, recording or otherwise), without the prior written permission of both the copyright owner and the publisher of this book. No paragraph of this publication may be reproduced, copied or transmitted save with written permission or in accordance with the provisions of the Copyright Act 1956 (as amended).

Also, by David Holding:

Murder in the Heather:
The Winter Hill Murder of 1838.

The Pendle Witch Trials of 1612.

The Dark Figure:
Crime in Victorian Bolton.

Bleak Christmas:
The Pretoria Colliery Disaster of 1910.

The Last Temptation:
The Trial of Doctor Harold Shipman.

All published by Scott Martin Productions, 2019.

John Bodkin Adams (1899-1983)

(Commons Attribution Photograph)

*Trial by jury is the lamp that
shows that freedom lives.*

Lord Patrick Devlin (1905-1992)

Acknowledgements

I am most grateful for the encouragement and support I have received from numerous quarters in the preparation of this work. In particular, I wish to express my sincere thanks to members of the medical and legal professions for the generous benefit of their experience, expertise and opinions on the many, and often emotive issues raised by this work. My thanks also go to those largely anonymous but ever obliging staff in the various institutions and libraries that I have consulted in my preparation for this work. Lastly, but by no mean least, I express my sincere gratitude to my publisher, Lesley Atherton, for her unfailing support and always helpful suggestions, and for keeping my feet firmly on the ground. My gratitude loses no sincerity in its generality.

The primary sources for this work have been R v Adams (1957) Trial Transcripts – National Archives, Criminal Law Review (1957) and Sybille Bedford's definitive verbatim account of the trial: 'The Best We Can Do'. In addition, a selection of other sources including books, legal and medical articles, and media reports have been consulted and acknowledged. I would, however, hasten to add, that none of the above are responsible for the contents of this work, and any errors are entirely my own.

David Holding, 2020

Contents

Acknowledgements 6
Introduction 9
Chapter One 15
    Early Years 15
Chapter Two 24
    The Police Investigation 24
Chapter Three 31
    The Trial 31
    Prosecution: Opening Address to the Jury 33
    Defence: Closing Address to the Jury 46
    Prosecution: Closing Address to the Jury: The Attorney General 51
    The Judge's Summing-Up to the Jury: Mr Justice Patrick Devlin 55
    The Post-Trial Period 64
Chapter Four 66
    An Overview of the Case 66
        The Case in Retrospect 66
        The Conduct of the Case 68
        The Police Investigation 70
        Suggestions of External Intervention in the Case 70
    Bibliographical Review on the Trial 73
        The Legal Position of the 'Double Effect' Principle 76
        Psychological Profile of Adams 80
        The Legal Issue of 'Causation' 88

Appendices 92
    Appendix A 92
        The Current Law of Homicide 92
    Appendix B 94
        'All I Tried To Do Was Relieve His Agony, His Distress And Suffering' 94
Selected Bibliography 97

Introduction

This book being the second of a trilogy, takes the reader into the private world of medical doctors and their practices. Each book has centred upon one individual doctor who was a general medical practitioner living and working in England during the period from the mid-1920s to 1999. Whilst each of these practitioners came from different backgrounds, there is one common thread running through their respective lives. They were all charged and stood trial for murder, yet their motives appear to have been different.

Motives ranged from the exercising of the ultimate power over life and death, the obsession with wealth, privilege and social acceptance, and finally revenge and jealousy.

Each case received widespread public attention at the time, and all have been the subjects of numerous books, articles and media attention. This book, together with its two companions, is innovative in that it approaches the subject of 'murder' in an entirely novel way.

Each work commences by describing the early background of the subject and their career development. I also look into the personal characteristics that may help to provide an insight into the possible motives for their later activities. The work then progresses to the criminal investigation and subsequent arrest, culminating in the trial. Each work concludes with a general overview of the case to draw together all the essential strands of the case. By adopting this approach, the author's intention has been to involve the reader in each case from the outset, rather than simply allow them to remain 'passive' observers to the events. As each case unfolds, the reader is taken on a chronological journey and presented with the relevant information relating to the case. When the trial itself is reached, all the evidence, both for the prosecution and defence is available for the reader to consider - as would be the case in the actual trial. To conclude, the reader is invited to consider their own verdict based on all the evidence available. In this way, the reader is able to exercise their own judgement in a practical, yet enjoyable, way. In so doing, it is hoped that these works will provide the reader with an insight into the often complex processes involved in criminal investigation and trials, and the workings of our Criminal Justice System.

    This second book of the trilogy centres on the trial of Dr John Bodkin Adams. Of Irish ancestry, this GP was based in Eastbourne, Sussex from the early 1920s. He was tried on one count of the murder of one of his elderly patients, Mrs Edith Alice Morrell, though the police claimed that Adams had also murdered a number of other elderly patients. They suggested that his 'modus operandi' was to administer the drugs, heroin and morphine, with the intention of making his patients addicts and therefore dependent upon him.

    He was then in a position to induce them to leave him legacies in cash and kind in their wills. This having been achieved, his final action was to give them large doses of opiate drugs which caused their deaths. It was later suggested by the trial judge, Devlin J. that the police became fixated on the idea that Adams had murdered many elderly patients for legacies, so much so that they regarded the evidence of these legacies as legitimate grounds for their suspicions. The police investigated the wills of 132 of Adams' former patients between 1946 and 1956, in which he had personally benefited from a legacy. A list of around twelve names was prepared and this was submitted to the Director of Public Prosecutions. Judge Devlin considered that Mrs Morrell's case, which was the one eventually chosen by the Attorney-General for prosecution, looked the strongest of the twelve submitted, although others involved in the investigation disagreed.

As outlined in the Attorney General's opening address to the jury, it was the case that Adams either administered or instructed others to administer drugs that killed Mrs Morrell with the 'intention' of killing her. Such drugs were unnecessary as she was not suffering pain because she had remained in a semi-comatose condition for some time prior to her death. The prosecution suggested as motive that Adams had decided it was time for Mrs Morrell to die because he feared that she may alter her will to his disadvantage. In strict law, the prosecution did not need to show a motive but, if no motive was provided, then the prosecution needed to prove the offence by determining precisely how the killing was carried out.

Throughout the trial, the prosecution maintained Adams' motive was essentially a mercenary one. However, the prosecution did not consider a possible alternative – that Adams intended 'euthanasia' – which could be implied from the comment he made on his arrest: 'I was easing the passing'.

The prosecution initially argued that the large quantities of morphia and heroin prescribed by Adams in the months leading up to Mrs Morrell's death, had all been injected into her. This amount, they insisted, was sufficient to kill her, and they also insisted that it could *only* have been intended to kill her.

Accordingly, Adams was accused of

murdering Mrs Morrell by one of two methods, singularly or in combination. The first alleged method was as a result of the accumulation of the amounts of opiates given in the ten months before her death. The second was the result of two large injections of an 'unknown' but prescribed lethal substance prepared by Adams and injected into Mrs Morrell shortly before her death.

However, on the second day of Adams' trial, the defence produced nurses' note-books, which clearly showed that much smaller quantities of drugs had been given to Mrs Morrell than those the prosecution had estimated, based on Adams' prescriptions. More significantly, these note-books also recorded that the two injections made the night before Mrs Morrell's death, were recorded as being of Paraldehyde, which was a very safe soporific.

In response to the defence's production of the nurses' note-books, one of the prosecution's expert medical witnesses changed his testimony from that he had given at Adams' pre-trial Committal Hearing. Dr Douthwaite had previously introduced a new theory on how he believed Mrs Morrell had been killed. This was not accepted by the prosecution's own second medical witness, nor indeed by the defence's medical expert witness. The prosecution's only reaction was to argue (unsuccessfully), that the nurses' note-books were incomplete.

However, this assertion led Judge Devlin to comment that by this point in the trial, a conviction seemed unlikely because the medical evidence was inconclusive.

In his summing-up, the Judge stated that a doctor 'had no special defence but he is entitled to do all that is proper and necessary to relieve pain even if the measures he takes may incidentally shorten life'.

This established the legal principle of 'Double Effect'.

The Judge also gave direction to the jury, that they should not conclude that any more drugs were administered to Mrs Morrell other than those shown in the nurses' note-books.

The Judge concluded by indicating to the jury that the main argument for the defence was that the whole case against Dr Adams rested on mere suspicion, and that the case for the defence 'seems to me to be a manifestly strong one'. On these grounds, the jury returned a Not Guilty verdict after deliberating for just forty-six minutes.

After his acquittal on the charge of murder, Bodkin Adams resigned from the National Health Service and in July 1957, he pleaded guilty to fourteen of the sixteen other charges against him for forging prescriptions, making false statements on Cremation Forms and being responsible for other offences under the Dangerous Drugs Act.

He was convicted of these offences and was consequently struck off the Medical Register but was reinstated in 1961.

He spent much of the rest of his life in pursuing his favourite hobby of clay pigeon shooting, together with undertaking limited research and consultancy work. He also continued to receive legacies from his former patients.

After complications following the breaking of his leg in 1983, he was admitted to Eastbourne General Hospital where he died of heart failure on 4th July 1983. He was cremated and his ashes interred in the grave of his parents back in Coleraine, Ireland.

John Bodkin Adams was undoubtedly an incompetent doctor with little understanding of the true nature of the drugs he supplied. However, he was not considered to have shown disregard for the accepted standards of medical practice of the time. In this respect, he was considered to be no better and no worse than his GP contemporaries.

He may well have been perceived as a greedy and acquisitive individual, but the 'evidence' supporting the numerous claims that he was a 'serial killer' really amounted to little more than unsubstantiated gossip and rumour.

Chapter One

Early Years

John Bodkin Adams was born 21st January 1899 in Randalstown, County Antrim, Northern Ireland and was given his mother's maiden name of Bodkin. His father, Samuel, was a local magistrate, watchmaker, jeweller and engineer by trade. Samuel and his wife Ellen had two sons, William and John, and they all later moved to Coleraine, where John attended the Academical Institution. His father died when he was 15 and his younger brother died in his teens in the 1918 influenza pandemic.

John Bodkin wasn't regarded as a particularly outstanding student but was described as 'hard-working'. He entered Queens University Belfast Medical School at the age of 17 and gained his MB, BCh and BAO degrees in 1921, qualifying as a medical doctor.

Following graduation, he met Professor Arthur Rendle Short, a surgeon, at a Belfast conference, and Short invited him to join his staff as a junior casualty officer at the Bristol Royal Infirmary in England.

During this time, he studied for a Diploma in Public Health (DPH). Wendell Short encouraged him to apply for a post as a junior general practitioner because a hospital career did not appeal. In 1922, Adams saw an advertisement for a Christian practice assistant GP in Eastbourne, Sussex, with the possibility of a partnership. Adams applied to the practice of Emerson, Gurney and Rainey, and was successful in being appointed.

Being a new GP, he had to buy into the practice for £2,000 which he raised by means of a secured bank loan. He was joined in Eastbourne by his mother and cousin, Sarah.

In a relatively small town like Eastbourne in the 1920s, a doctor had a standing in the local community, because of his close and special relationship with his patients. Once established in the town, he immersed himself in the 'social' life of the town by joining the Eastbourne Medical Society. He also organised Young Crusader's Bible Classes and was a supporter of Holy Trinity Church in the town.

The start of a fruitful relationship began when he was called to the mansion of William Mawhood, a wealthy retired steel merchant. His wife Edith had injured her leg and Adams referred her to a London surgeon who operated on it. The Mawhoods had a large home and land, even a gamekeeper for their estate. Adams was invited to join the pheasant shoots because he was a champion shot and as such, was welcomed into the 'country set'. Over time, he added many of the Sussex gentry to his patient list.

Within two years of joining the practice, Adams bought his first car and soon became an enthusiastic motorist and keen photographer. For four years he undertook research for his doctorate in Public Health which then enabled him to become a full partner in the practice in 1926, improving his financial status.

In 1929, a Victorian villa named Kent Lodge, went on the market and Adams was very impressed with it, since it had been a doctor's surgery in the 1880s. To purchase it, he borrowed most of the £3,000 required from William Mawhood, and also spent £2,000 of his own savings to convert the property. Around the time of Christmas 1930, he moved in with his mother, cousin Sarah, a servant and a chauffeur. On the social scene, Adams became a founding member of the Bisley Rifle Club and a local camera club. He was introduced to Lt Colonel Roland Gwynne, a man of great wealth and social influence in Sussex, who was chairman of the Eastbourne bench of magistrates. To be in with the Colonel was to be part of the 'jet set' of the county – a group of men of wealth and influence with many contacts.

However, whilst Adams was certainly attracted by the high life, he did not forget his patients. He prospered and was popular with both his 'panel' (NHS) and private patients and never refused to visit patients at home.

Having obtained his Diploma in Anaesthetics (DA), Adams was appointed as part-time anaesthetist at the Princess Alice Memorial Hospital, Eastbourne in 1941. By the mid-1930s, Adams had a practice of 2,000 patients, around 1,000 'panel-patients' and the rest private. Panel-patients were working men who contributed to a national fund at work which paid the GP – this was a scheme introduced in 1910 by the prime minister, Lloyd George. Like most doctors at the time, Adams tailored his charges to the patients' financial state, in fact often not charging the very poor families at all.

However, by 1935, rumours began to circulate around the town regarding Adams' practices. A wealthy widow, Mrs Matilda Whitton, had been one of Adam's patients, and a friendly relationship developed between patient and doctor. When Mrs Whitton became incapable of driving herself, Adams would loan her his car and chauffeur.

As with most of Adams' activities, the motives could be interpreted in different ways. It could be argued that his kindly activities were in his patients' best interests, or that they were done with the intention of being remembered in her will.

However, he was legitimately entitled to be appointed as Mrs Whitton's executor since none of her immediate family lived in Eastbourne. When she died of high blood pressure on 11th May 1935 at the age of 75, she left him £7,000 and also left £500 to his cousin. She also provided a codicil which bequeathed £100 to his mother, and the estate's total was around £200,000 by today's standards.

Mrs Whitton's family contested the will, although the High Court upheld it, quashing only the codicil. The publicity caused much local gossip, and some believe this to be the first of many adverse criticisms concerning Adams' character.

As early as the late 1930s, rumours were rife in Eastbourne about Adams receiving bequests and, more significantly, about the manner in which certain of his patients had died. It also appears that, at this time, there was much jealousy and envy among competing general practitioners in the town, with Adams becoming the most unpopular doctor there.

Another of Adams' failings was that he rarely kept records of his patients' details or of the drugs he prescribed, which did indicate a certain laxity in his administrative skills.

Also, it has been estimated that Adams' practice income was in the range of £7,000 a year. His private patients included nobility such as the Duke of Devonshire, the Sheriff of the County, Sir Roland Gwynne, and Richard Walker, the Chief Constable of Eastbourne. As a result of these patients, Adams was rapidly becoming the talk of Eastbourne. However, unlike other professionals, Adams had an unhealthy tendency to boast about his practices and was certainly ostentatious about his wealth. His partners were also critical of his excessive use of dangerous drugs and expressed their concerns to him.

Adams stayed in Eastbourne throughout the war, and he was described as being 'furious' at not being deemed desirable by other local doctors to be selected for a 'pool system' in which general practitioners in the town would treat patients of the doctors who had been called up for military service.

In 1941, Adams gained his Diploma in Anaesthetics which enabled him to work on a part-time basis at the Princess Alice Memorial Hospital in Eastbourne. In 1943, his mother died, followed in 1952 by his cousin Sarah who developed cancer. It is believed that Adams gave her an injection half an hour before she died, this being the only case where it could be considered that the doctor was 'easing the passing'.

Adam's career was very successful and by 1956, he was possibly one of the wealthiest GPs in the area. Whilst there were criticisms regarding Adams' overall competence, most observers agreed that he did appear to have an excellent bedside manner, particularly with his mostly elderly patients.

Over the succeeding years he built up a lucrative private practice attending to the needs of the many wealthy patients who had retired to the south coast, and many of them seemed to be grateful for his kind attentions.

Including a legacy for their doctors was not unusual in patients' wills. Adams received fourteen legacies totalling £21,000 from his former patients. As a doctor in receipt of such amounts, he soon became the subject of the usual gossip in the town, with various 'unsubstantiated' rumours circulating. One rumour was that the doctor had been responsible for the deaths, and that he his motive was the receipt of legacies.

One of Adam's patients, Gertrude Joyce

Hullett, suffered from depression following the death of her second husband, Alfred John Hullett, in 1956. Adams prescribed her barbiturates or 'barbitones' as they were known at the time, in order to help her sleep.

On the 22nd July 1956, Mrs Hullett lapsed into unconsciousness and Adams thought that she had suffered a brain haemorrhage or stroke. He immediately contacted the Coroner to arrange the necessary post-mortem. However, when the Coroner discovered to his obvious amazement and annoyance, that Mrs Hullett was still alive, he accused Adams of 'extreme incompetence'.

Despite this 'false alarm', Gertrude Hullett died the following day, and' although Adams recorded the cause of death as having been the result of a brain haemorrhage, the post-mortem revealed that she had in fact died after taking an overdose of barbiturates.

The subsequent Inquest held on 21st August, concluded that she had committed suicide 'of her own free will' as evidence had been provided that she'd repeatedly confided in her solicitor and friends that she intended to take her own life. However, the East Sussex Coroner, Dr AC Somerville, did note that Gertrude had experienced 'an extraordinary amount of careless treatment', and that the doctors attending her had failed to realise they were dealing with a case of barbiturate poisoning until it was too late to administer the antidote.

It was also noted that Adams had been left a Rolls Royce car in Gertrude's will and had also received a cheque for £1,000 only days before her death, and that Adams had requested the bank process this cheque with special clearance. It was at this time that Eastbourne police received an anonymous call claiming that Adams was responsible for turning Gertrude Hullett into a 'drug addict'.

The first unusual feature of the Inquest Hearing was the appearance of a Detective Superintendent Herbert Hannam from Scotland Yard. He was asked by the Coroner if there were any reasons why the Inquest should be adjourned. The Coroner explained that the Chief Constable of Eastbourne had requested the aid of Scotland Yard to investigate certain 'suspicious' deaths that had occurred in the neighbourhood. It remained uncertain why the Chief Constable decided to take this step, or why he thought it appropriate for this decision to be announced during the course of the Inquest into what appeared to be a straightforward case of suicide.

The second unusual feature of the Hearing was the extraordinary amount of interest being shown by the national press in what otherwise would have been an unremarkable Inquest. It became obvious that the press had been 'tipped off' that there was a potential story worth following in Eastbourne.

On the 22nd of August 1956, *The Daily Mail* ran a report of the Hullett Inquest under the headline: 'Yard Probes Mass Poisonings: Twenty Five Deaths in the Great Mystery of Eastbourne'. Although this report did not mention Adams by name, it became quite obvious that the article was referring to him.

This was followed with further press headlines such as: 'Enquiry into Four Hundred Wills: Rich Women Believed to Have been the Victims' appearing in *The Daily Telegraph*.

This gave the general impression that there was a mass murderer on the loose on the south coast, which certainly warranted police attention. It also appears that there was a confidential meeting at the Princes Alice Hospital in 1954 concerning certain aspects of Dr Adams' practices.

It was believed that Dr Adams might be forging doctors' signatures in order to procure NHS Services for his private patients. This resulted in a cloud of suspicion and gossip hanging over Adams throughout the 1950s. The gossip mainly concerned the number of patients who had left money to him, and, while it had to be admitted that Eastbourne with its significantly high population of elderly people could expect a correspondingly high death rate, the rumours questioned how often patients leaving him legacies had died.

Whilst it could be expected that some of these deaths would be sudden, the question did arise: Were these deaths, in fact, being hastened by Adams?

Readers were informed that the Scotland Yard murder squad was investigating the suspected poisoning of hundreds of wealthy women in Eastbourne over a period of 20 years. As a result, detectives embarked on an investigation of Dr Adams' professional life, their brief being to look for any evidence of fraud and murder.

Eventually, a picture emerged of Dr Adams as a greedy, avaricious physician of dubious morality: an insatiable legacy hunter.

This view was fuelled by statements from solicitors and bank managers testifying to Dr Adams' persistence in pressing patients to alter their wills in his favour.

A painstaking search found 132 wills containing £45,000 in bequests to the doctor (a very large sum for the time). Cases were discovered of cremation forms in which the doctor had failed to declare his interest as a beneficiary under the will – an intentional omission that avoided the need for a post-mortem examination.

A study of the doctor's death certificates also raised questions about his diagnostic capability or honesty, since an unnaturally high proportion had 'cerebral haemorrhage' or 'cerebral thrombosis' entered as the cause of death.

Instances of sudden decline and death following closely after a will change excited particular interest, especially from the police.

Relatives also drew the Yard's attention to the case of 82 year-old Julia Bradnum, who died with unexpected suddenness in 1952, leaving the doctor as sole executor of a new will. The Yard subsequently exhumed her body. They also exhumed the bodies of the Mss Hilda and Clara Neil Miller, spinster sisters who died in 1953 and 1954. Hilda left everything to Clara, and Clara left most of her estate to Adams.

In late October 1956, Hannam submitted his dossier on the investigation into Adams' activities to Sir Theobald Matthew, the Director of Public Prosecutions.

Chapter Two

The Police Investigation

The investigation had been taken over from Eastbourne police on the 17th August 1956 by two officers from the Metropolitan Police's Murder Squad. The senior officer was Detective Superintendent Herbert Hannam of Scotland Yard who was known for having solved the Teddington towpath murders in 1953. He was assisted by Detective Sergeant Charles Hewett, and Inspector Brynley Pugh as liaison officer from Eastbourne police.

Hannam was in an unusual position. Instead of having to find a suspect for a known case, he already had a suspect in Dr Adams. However, he needed to link him to more offences of a more serious nature than forging prescriptions, making false statements on cremation forms and mishandling dangerous drugs. In pursuance of this, Hannam launched a detailed investigation into Dr Adam's professional activities in Eastbourne. It has been suggested that Hannam became fixated with the belief that Adams had murdered many elderly patients for legacies. However, his main ground for suspicion was that Adams had received several legacies but in reality, these were only as a minor beneficiary.

It was arranged for the Home Office pathologist, Dr Francis Camps, to examine 310 death certificates certified by Adams over a ten year period from 1946 to 1956. Camps considered that a total of 143 (46%) of these were 'suspicious'. He also highlighted the fact that a high proportion of these certificates certified death as due to 'cerebral haemorrhage' or 'cerebral thrombosis'. The police took numerous statements from the nurses who had treated Adams' patients. Some of these were favourable to him, whilst others claimed that Adams had given patients 'special' injections of 'unknown substances' which Adams refused to describe to the nurses.

These statements also claimed that his habit was to ask the nurses to leave the room before the injections were given. He would also isolate patients from their relatives preventing contact between them, and this was a rather unusual practice.

On the 24th August 1956, the British Medical Association (BMA), sent a letter to all doctors in Eastbourne reminding them of 'patient confidentiality' if they were interviewed by the police. Hannam regarded this as 'obstructing' his investigation. He, together with the Attorney General, Sir Reginald Mannigham-Buller, wrote to the secretary of the BMA urging him to remove this ban on police interviewing. However, it was not until 8th November that the Attorney General met with the BMA secretary personally and convinced him of the importance of the case being investigated. It also appears that during this meeting, he passed Hannam's report on Adams to the secretary.

It is very likely that this report was copied and found its way into the hands of Adams' defence team, before being returned at day later, to the Attorney-General's office. This in itself, was a very unprecedented move for a prosecutor to make, given the confidentiality of the file. Now convinced of the seriousness of the accusations levelled at Adams, the BMA secretary dropped his opposition to doctors being interviewed by the police.

Hannam came to the conclusions that he was 'confident' that Adams was a 'mass-murderer' and that he had certainly killed at least fourteen people. Rather unprofessionally for an investigating detective, Hannam is believed to have also passed this information to the 'ever listening' members of the press who had now descended on Eastbourne in their droves. Hannam based his 'theory' on the fact that Dr Adams made his victims dependant on drugs, persuaded them to change their wills in his favour, and then killed them with an overdose.

How much this theory was based on reliable or 'circumstantial' evidence or entirely on rumour and gossip, is anyone's guess.

In pursuance of his theory, Hannam contrived a meeting with Adams on 1st October 1956 by deliberately walking past his home with the specific intention of engaging Adams in conversation. During this conversation, Hannam raised the matter of the legacy that Adams had received from Mrs Edith Morrell – one of his patients. In particular, Hannam wanted to know why Adams had not declared that he was a beneficiary under her will on her cremation form – a form which he had completed and signed.

Adams's response to this was that it was 'not done wickedly but simply to allow the cremation to go smoothly for the sake of the relatives and it was not deceitful'. Hannam also mentioned to Adams that he had forged a prescription for drugs, to which Adams admitted 'it was wrong of me to do that'.

As a result of this 'unofficial' conversation, Hannam now established that he had evidence that there were indeed irregularities in Adams' professional activities. As a result, the police obtained a warrant under the Dangerous Drugs Act 1951, and arrested Adams on the 24th November 1956, and executed a search of his home and surgery. This search was undertaken by Superintendent Hannam and Inspector Pugh, head of Eastbourne CID. They explained to Adams that they were looking for morphine, heroin and pethidine drugs.

Adams' reply was that they would not find any in the house because he seldom used them. Hannam then asked Adams for his Dangerous Drugs Register which records drugs ordered and used by the doctor. His reply was 'I keep no register and have not kept one since 1949'.

When Hannam showed Adams a list of dangerous drugs which he had prescribed for his patient Mrs Morrell, and asked who administered them, Adams replied, 'I did nearly all. Perhaps the nurses gave some but mostly me'.

Hannam then pointed out, 'Doctor, you prescribed for her 75-1/6 grains of heroin tablets the day before she died'.

Adams replied, 'Poor soul, she was in such agony. It was all used, I used them myself'.

As a result of the search on 24th November 1956, Adams was taken to Eastbourne Police station where he was charged with eight offences under the Forgery Act 1913, four under the Cremation Act 1902 and one under the Larceny Act 1956.

The majority of the charges related to the forging of National Health Service prescriptions, whilst the charges under the Cremation Act related to the fact that he had made false representations on death certificates stating that he had 'no pecuniary interest in the deceased's estate' – a statement which he knew to be false.

On the 26th of November, Adams appeared at Eastbourne Magistrates' Court where he was remanded on bail of £2,000 and required to surrender his passport. Whilst at the police station Superintendent Hannam informed Adams that they were looking into the death of a number of his patients and in particular, Mrs Morrell. Adams' reply was: 'Easing the passing of a dying person is not all that wicked. She wanted to die. That cannot be murder. It is impossible to accuse a doctor'.

On the 19th December 1956, Adams was arrested a second time, charged with the murder of Edith Alice Morrell on a day in November 1950. Adams' reply to the charge was: 'Murder? Can you prove it was murder? I did not think you could prove murder. She was dying in any event'.

The police also charged Adams with two further charges under the Dangerous Drugs Act 1951 relating to his attempt to conceal drugs and obstructing the police during the search of his home, together with failing to keep a register of drugs as required under the Dangerous Drugs Regulations 1953. Adams was remanded in Brixton Prison to await the Committal Hearing.

The original list of cases that Hannam regarded as warranting prosecution was narrowed down to those of Mrs Morrell, Mr & Mrs Hullett, Clara Neil Miller and Julia Bradnum.

However, in the cases of Mr Hullett, Clara Miller and Julia Bradnum, there was no certainty of an unnatural death as there was evidence that Mr Hullett died of a heart attack.

As a result of the exhumations of Miss Miller, the pathologist concluded that she died of pneumonia.

The condition of Bradnum's body did not allow a cause of death to be stated.

Mrs Hullett had died an unnatural death of barbiturate overdose, but there was no evidence or admission that Adams had persuaded to take the overdose.

The Committal Hearing opened in Lewes on

the 14th January 1957.

Adams was charged on the single count of murdering Mrs Morrell, although the prosecution also alleged that he had killed Mr and Mrs Hullett in a similar fashion. They introduced evidence relating to them as 'similar fact' evidence. Despite the objections of the defence team that this type of evidence was inadmissible, the magistrates allowed it. However, in cross-examination, the defence did force an admission from the Crown's expert witness, that Mr Hullett had died of a coronary thrombosis.

The defence made an application for the Committal Hearing to be held in private, believing it would be prejudicial for the defence to have the prosecution evidence on the Hullet case made public, when Adams was only facing the charge of murdering Edith Morrell. However, this was refused.

The Hearing lasted nine days, concluding on the 24th January with Adams being committed for trial on the Morrell charge. The Chairman of the magistrates was Sir Roland Gwynne, but he stepped down because of his close relationship with Adams.

A vital piece of evidence (the cheque written out by Mrs Hullett for £1,000) went missing after the hearing. While the culprit was never found, Scotland Yard suspected the Deputy Chief Constable of Eastbourne of having misplaced in an attempt to help Adams. He was known to have taken holidays with Adams and Gwynne.

Mr Justice Devlin, the trial judge offered the opinion later that it would have been wiser if the Committal Hearing had been in private.

Adams was returned to Brixton Prison to await trial. Following the Committal Hearing, the Attorney General informed the trial judge, that he would not be using the evidence regarding Mr Hullett in the Morrell trial but would seek a second indictment relating to Mrs Hullett, which he did on the 5th March 1957. Had he proceeded with a second indictment, then a second committal hearing would have been required. Consequently, the indictment relating to Mrs Hullett would have been held back for a possible second trial.

Chapter Three

The Trial

R v ADAMS

CENTRAL CRIMINAL COURT, LONDON, BEFORE MR JUSTICE PATRICK DEVLIN.

CHARGED WITH THE MURDER OF EDITH ALICE MORRELL ON THE 13TH DAY OF NOVEMBER 1950.

PLEADED: NOT GUILTY.

PROSECUTING COUNSEL: DEFENCE COUNSEL:

Sir Reginald Manningham-Buller, QC, MP.
Mr Geoffrey Lawrence, QC.
Mr Melford Stevenson, QC.
Mr Edward Clarke QC.
Mr Malcolm Morris.
Mr John Heritage.

    Dr Adams faced two charges, firstly that he murdered Mrs Morrell and secondly that he murdered Mr & Mrs Hullett.
    Following legal precedent, he first faced the charge of murdering Mrs Morrell. The case was heard at the Old Bailey in London, and the Medical Defence Union (MDU) had chosen Geoffrey Lawrence QC – a very skilful and persuasive barrister – to defend him.

The essence of the prosecution case was that an eighty-one year-old woman, half paralysed by a stroke, had died. The prosecution maintained that her death was not the result of age or illness but of poisoning by drugs. These drugs, they maintained, were prescribed during the last five days of her life without a medical reason.

The weight of the prosecution case rested on three pertinent questions.

Firstly, was the quantity of drugs prescribed actually administered and by whom?

Secondly, was the dosage of the drugs actually fatal or merely excessively large?

Thirdly, was there in fact, no medical reason other than murder to account for their administration?

According to Sybille Bedford's astute observation:

'Yet in a way the motive has already drawn sustenance from an irregular but not secret source; it has waxed big by headlines, by printed innuendo, by items half remembered from the committal hearing. There have been published rumours of rich patients, mass poisonings, of legacy on legacy in solid sterling. Everybody knows a bit too much and no one knows quite enough; there is a most disturbing element in this case, extra-mural, half-knowledge that cannot be admitted and cannot be kept out.'
The Best We Can Do (1989) p 24.

Described by Rupert Furneux in his *Famous Criminal Cases*, the trial of Adams was considered to be 'one of the greatest murder trials of all time', and by *The Times* as 'the murder trial of the century'.

The trial was presided over by Mr Justice Patrick Devlin (later Lord), who noted that the case presented the 'most curious situation' which was 'perhaps unique in these courts, that the act of murder has to be proved by expert evidence'.

The trial lasted seventeen days which, at the time, made it the longest murder trial in English criminal history. What Judge Devlin meant by his remarks was that the first task of the prosecution was to convince the jury that Edith Alice Morrell had in fact been murdered. This was a far from straightforward task, since they had no body, and since the formal cause of death had already been recorded as cerebral thrombosis by the very same doctor now being accused of murdering her.

Essentially, the prosecution argument was that Mrs Morrell had in fact died as a result of the various drugs given to her by Adams. In order to demonstrate this, the prosecution relied firstly on the testimony of the nurses who attended Mrs Morrell during her last days. They were questioned on the drugs they actually administered to her on Adam's instructions, and secondly on the expert medical evidence that it was this course of drugs that killed Edith Morrell.

Prosecution: Opening Address to the Jury

Opening the case for the prosecution, the Attorney General, Sir Reginald Manningham-Buller described Dr Adams to the jury as a doctor in his fifties who was charged with the murder of one of his patients, the murder occurring six years ago. He was a Doctor of Medicine and Bachelor of Surgery, with a Diploma in Anaesthetics. The victim was described as an eighty-one year old widow who left an estate valued at £157,000. She died in November 1950 having suffered a stroke two years earlier, the result of which left her paralysed. Adams was the doctor in charge of her care.

In addition, Mrs Morrell was attended to by four nurses who would give evidence that they never saw Mrs Morrell suffering from severe pain. The prosecution would be calling a Harley Street consultant who would confirm that, in his opinion, Mrs Morrell was suffering from cerebral arteriole-sclerosis or 'hardening of the arteries'. The jury would also be told of large quantities of drugs prescribed and administered by Adams over the course of months.

One of the questions to be considered was why were they given? The total quantity of the drugs given over a period of ten and a half months amounted to: 1,629 grains of barbiturates; 1,928 grains of Sedormid; 164 grains of morphia and 130 grains of heroin. The jury was informed that if these drugs were administered over a significant period of time, they would result in a 'serious degree of addiction' and a dependence on them. Since Dr Adams was the source of this supply, it follows that Mrs Morrell must have become dependent upon him. Another question arose of why these drugs were prescribed to an old lady who was not suffering from pain.

The jury was then informed that Mrs Morrell made three wills in 1947 in which Dr Adams was not mentioned. Then in April 1949 when Mrs Morrell had been receiving both morphia and heroin for several months, Dr Adams contacted her solicitor, Mr Sogro, to express concerns that Mrs Morrell was very anxious about her will and that she required to see him urgently.

The solicitor attended Mrs Morrell which resulted in her making another will in which she bequeathed Dr Adams an oak chest containing silver. After a period of almost twelve months,

Adams again visited Mr Sogro to inform him that Mrs Morrell had promised him her Rolls Royce car in her will, but that she had forgotten to include this in her latest version, together with the contents of a box deposited with her bank. Adams stressed to the solicitor that despite Mrs Morrell's illness, her mind was perfectly clear and that she was in a fit state to execute a codicil to her will.

Having reservations about this, Mr Sogro insisted that they should wait until Mrs Morrell's son came to visit her. Despite this, Adams suggested that the solicitor should prepare a codicil which could be executed but destroyed if it did not meet with the approval of Mrs Morrell's son. This resulted in Mr Sogro visiting Mrs Morrell once again, when she made another will in which she left Adams the chest of silver but left him the Rolls Royce car only on the condition that her son pre-deceased her.

In September of 1949, Dr Adams was away on holiday and Mrs Morrell was attended by Adams' partner, Dr Harris. Mrs Morrell was so annoyed with this that she executed yet another codicil to her last will, this time revoking her entire bequests to Adams.

At this point, the Attorney General then produced a graph showing the alleged prescriptions issued by Dr Adams which indicated how the rates of morphia had increased three times during the final thirteen days of Mrs Morrell's life, far more than at any time during the previous months, with the rate of heroin increasing by seven and a half times.

The Attorney General then raised the question of what had happened to Mrs Morrell that made it necessary for these large increases. He suggested that if she had been in severe pain, these increases could have been justified, but said that she was not in pain.

The jury were then informed that the nurses

who attended Mrs Morrell would confirm that during her final days, Mrs Morrell was in fact, in a semi-conscious state (a coma). The Attorney General continued: 'Why did the doctor prescribe such quantities for which there was no medical justification? The submission of the Crown is that he did so because he had decided that the time had come for Mrs Morrell to die'.

Describing the night of her death, the prosecution said that Mrs Morrell was lying unconscious in a coma. At 10 pm, Dr Adams filled a 5cc syringe with a 'preparation' and instructed the night nurse to inject it into the unconscious patient, which she did. The doctor then refilled the empty syringe with another large quantity, instructing the nurse to give this second injection if the patient did not become quieter. The nurse gave the second injection, and at 2 am, Mrs Morrell died.

The jury was then asked to consider the question of why such large injections were given to an unconscious woman? The prosecution did concede that Mrs Morrell may well have been a dying woman when the injections were given. That being the case, the prosecution submitted that she was, in effect, dying from overdoses of morphia and heroin, prescribed by Dr Adams, this constituting murder by the doctor.

Similarly, if the two injections did in fact accelerate death, this also constituted murder. The Attorney General then told the jury: 'The prosecution will submit that the only conclusion to which you can come is that the doctor killed her, deliberately and intentionally'.

The prosecution then told the jury that on the same day that Mrs Morrell died, the 13th November 1950, Adams filled in the form to secure Mrs

Morrell's cremation. To the question on the form: 'Have you, as far as you are aware, any pecuniary interest in the death of the deceased?' Adams wrote 'Not as far as I am aware'. Consequently, authority was given for Mrs Morrell's cremation.

In 1956, when police from Scotland Yard were making inquiries, the detective superintendent in charge of the investigation questioned Adams about this cremation certificate. Adams' reply was: 'Oh, that was not done wickedly. God knows it wasn't. We always want cremations to go off smoothly for the dear relatives. If I had said I knew I was getting money under the will, they might get suspicious, and I like cremations and burials to go off smoothly. There was nothing suspicious really. It was not deceitful'.

In November 1956, Detective Superintendent Hannam together with two other detectives visited Dr Adams at his home to execute a search warrant for dangerous drugs. The Superintendent asked Adams to look at a list of prescriptions he had made out for Mrs Morrell, with the comment: 'There are a lot of dangerous drugs here. Who administered them?'

Adams' reply was 'I did, nearly all. Perhaps the nurses gave some, but mostly me'. The Superintendent then asked Adams a further question: 'Were there any of these drugs left over when she died?' to which Adams answered: 'No none, all was given to the patient. Poor soul was in terrible agony.'

The prosecution then reminded the jury that the maximum quantity of heroin which should be prescribed in any period of twenty-four hours is ¼ of a grain. No less than eight grains were prescribed by Adams on one single day alone. The maximum dose of morphia recommended is ½ grain. Yet, between the 8th and 11th of November, a total of 40 grains were prescribed. Expert medical witnesses would confirm that Mrs Morrell could not survive the administration of those drugs during her final days.

The Attorney General concluded his opening speech to the jury by relating the fact that Dr Adams visited Detective Superintendent Hannam to inquire on the progress of the police investigation. He was informed by the superintendent that he was still inquiring into the death of some of his patients.

The doctor asked which patients he was referring to, and the superintendent replied: 'Mrs Morrell is certainly one'. To this, Dr Adams replied: 'Easing the passing of a dying person is not all that wicked. She wanted to die, that cannot be murder. It is impossible to accuse a doctor'.

In December 1956, Dr Adams was arrested and informed that he was being charged with the murder of Mrs Morrell. To this, Adams replied: 'Murder, can you prove it was murder?'

The superintendent then informed Dr Adams 'You are now charged with murder' to which Adams replied: 'I do not think you could prove it was murder, she was dying in any event'.

The prosecution concluded: 'I submit to you that the evidence I and my learned friends will call before you, will prove conclusively that this old lady was murdered'.

To summarise the prosecution case, an eighty-one year old woman, paralysed after a stroke had died. It was the prosecution's submission that she did not die of illness or of natural causes, but as the result of drugs prescribed during the final five days of her life.

According to Sybille Bedford: 'Three pertinent questions arose in relation to the prosecution case. Was the quantity of drugs prescribed actually

administered? Was the dosage of these drugs actually fatal or was it merely very large? And, was there in fact, no medical or other reason short of murder for their administration?
The Best We Can Do by Sybille Bedford, Penguin Books, Harmondsworth (1989) p23

To support the first strand of their case, the prosecution produced four witnesses in the form of the nurses who had attended Mrs Morrell in her final days, Helen Stronach, Helen Mason-Ellis, Caroline Randall and Brenda Bartlett. Nurse Helen Stronach, the first to take the witness stand, stated that at 9 pm she gave Mrs Morrell ¼ grain of morphia, then at 11 pm the doctor would give another injection but that she did not know what it was. Defence counsel, Geoffrey Lawrence QC asked if she had written these occurrences in the nurses report book, to which she replied: 'Yes, every time we gave an injection, we wrote it down, what it was, the time it was administered and our names'. Lawrence then suggested that 'anything and everything that happened of significance in the patient's illness would have to go down in these books?'

Nurse Stronach replied: 'We reported everything'.

Lawrence continued with his cross-examination. 'So that if only we had those reports now, we could see the truth of exactly what happened, night by night and day by day when you were there?' Nurse Stronach confirmed 'Yes'.

To everyone's complete surprise, Lawrence produced the nurses' note-books and asked Nurse Stronach to identify them. It was widely believed that such note-books had been destroyed after the patient's death.

Lawrence then proceeded to read out the entries that Nurse Stronach had to admit she had made. He then concluded his cross-examination of this prosecution witness: 'We have now been through the whole of your records for that time. We have not found a single instance where you gave that injection of ¼ grain of morphia by itself that you have been talking about. You recorded only one or two visits by the Doctor, and then we find you knew exactly what the injection was that was administered'.

Nurse Stronach had no comment to make on these revelations, Lawrence having effectively demolished her credibility. She was followed onto the witness stand by Sister Mason-Ellis, who, by now, was acutely aware of the existence of the note-books.

In cross examination of this witness, Lawrence read out her report for the afternoon preceding Mrs Morrell's death. This stated: 'Awake but quiet. Half a glass of milk and brandy, 3 drachms taken'.

Mr Lawrence continued: 'This indicates quite clearly that she was not in a coma'. In response to this revelation, Sister Mason-Ellis replied: 'Not according to my report'. To this, Lawrence replied: 'Did you not agree that the reports were where the truth was to be found? You do not want to go back on that now, do you?' Her reply was: 'Not at all'. Lawrence further replied: 'So when you wrote "awake" she must have been awake?' to which Sister Mason-Ellis replied that 'She must have been'. Finally, Lawrence concluded his cross examination of this witness with the comment: 'Therefore she could not possibly have been in a coma'.

Nurse Randall followed onto the witness stand, having been regarded as the prosecution's 'star' witness, because she had been present with Mrs

Morrell during the final hours prior to her death.

The Attorney General had highlighted in his opening address to the jury that she would describe this crucial period in detail to them: 'The night nurse will tell you Mrs Morrell was very weak, except for occasional spasms, she was in a coma. At 10 pm the Doctor came and himself filled a 5cc syringe with a preparation'.

Holding up an empty 5cc syringe to the jury, the Attorney General stated that the doctor gave this syringe to the night nurse and told her to inject the contents into the unconscious woman, which she did. The doctor took the empty syringe and refilled it with a similar quantity which was far too large a quantity on each occasion to be morphine or heroin, and he told the nurse to give the second injection to the patient if she did not become quieter.

The nurse did not like giving another large injection from this unusually large syringe – whatever it was – and later in the evening, she telephoned the doctor. She received instructions and it was her duty to obey them. So, she gave the second injection, Mrs Morrell gradually became quiet, and at 2 am she died. The prosecution cannot tell you what was in the syringes.

The Attorney General did not ask this witness to repeat the evidence she had given at Dr Adams' Committal Hearing, because her 'written' report told a very different story to her 'verbal' one. In cross examination of this witness, Lawrence read out the entries from the report-book: 'Patient very weak and restless. 9.30 pm 'Paraldehyde' 5cc given intravenously by the Doctor. 11.30 pm, very restless no sleep. 12.30 am, restless and talkative and very shaky. 12.45 am seems a little quieter, appears asleep, respiration 50. 2 am passed away quietly."

There were no references made to 'spasms', no injections given by the nurse, no phone calls, one injection given by the Doctor; when the patient was not unconscious but restless, not with a lethal dose of powerful morphine or heroin, but a reasonable dose of safe, paraldehyde. Nurse Randall, in her original evidence to the Committal Hearing said that she had telephoned the doctor and given a second injection. However, Lawrence now in cross examination asked: 'Why give the injection when the patient was not restless but quieter and seemed asleep? Your memory isn't very trustworthy?' to which Nurse Randall replied: 'It appears not to be'.

It is apparent that the prosecution had led Nurse Randall to describe Mrs Morrell's jerky spasms because these were a common sign of a withdrawal symptom from opiate poisoning, the main contention of the prosecution's case. Still under cross examination by the defence, Nurse Randall continued: 'They were so bad I could not leave her, and they almost jerked her out of bed. I have never seen jerks as bad'.

In response, Lawrence commented that they were not bad enough to be recorded in her report, to which Nurse Randall replied: 'I wrote that she was very shaky'. Lawrence responded: 'Shaky? Was that the word for the spasms that almost jerked the patient out of bed?' to which the nurse replied: 'I just don't know. I suppose I wrote it down quickly'.

Answering a question from the judge, Nurse Randall stated: 'I think 4cc or 5cc of paraldehyde is a very large dose'. Lawrence then informed her: 'Do you know that the British Pharmacopoeia full dose is 120 minims or 8cc?'

The fourth and final nurse to take the witness stand was Sister Brenda Bartlett, who had shared the last night duty with Nurse Randall. She began by repeating some of the evidence she too had given at Adams' Committal Hearing. She told that the patient had 'twitching spasms and was semi-comatose'.

Once again, Lawrence read out her written report: 'Awake, restless, talkative', to which Lawrence commented: 'This was hardly semi-comatose, not a spasm, twitch or shake'. It soon became obvious that the prosecution had expected the nurses' evidence to be undisputed. However, with the report books, Lawrence had been able to challenge the prosecution evidence, point by point, and in effect, destroying it over a period of one week.

The next prosecution witness was Dr Arthur Henry Douthwaite, senior physician at Guy's Hospital, London, the first of their medical expert witnesses. Like the nurses, he too, had given evidence previously at Adams' Committal Hearing and expected to be asked to repeat this same evidence at the trial. To reiterate the Attorney General's intention in his opening speech to the jury: 'The prosecution will call a medical authority who will tell you that in their view Mrs Morrell could not possibly have survived the administration of the drugs prescribed for her in the last five days of her life'.

However, that evidence was now challenged because the nurses' note-books indicated that Mrs Morrell had, in effect, been given only a small proportion of the drugs prescribed for her at the end.

Doughwaite stated that he believed Bodkin Adams must have meant murder if he gave his patient 41 grains of morphia and 39 grains of heroin in her last five days. However, the evidence proved otherwise. According to the prosecution chemist's calculations, the discrepancy between prescription and administration during the period, was 30 grains of morphia and 22 grains of heroin. In view of these significantly revised figures, together with the nurses' note-books, could Dr Douthwaite still maintain that he believed Dr Adams was trying to kill his patient?

Was he, in effect, influenced by prosecution lawyers to give evidence they so badly needed to keep the case going?

The Attorney General asked Dr Douthwaite: 'Is there, in your opinion, any justification for injecting morphia and heroin immediately after a stroke?' The doctor replied: 'No justification whatsoever'. The Attorney General continued: 'Is it right or wrong to do so?' and Dr Douthwaite answered: 'Wrong in all circumstances, wrong'. Finally, the Attorney General asked Dr Douthwaite: 'What conclusion do you draw from the dosage administered in the last days, and what conclusions do you draw as to the intentions with which that dosage must have been prescribed?' Dr Douthwaite replied: 'The only conclusion I can come to is that the intention on 8 November was to terminate her life'.

Dr Douthwaite had been incorrect in assuming, when he gave his evidence at the Committal Hearing that for the last three or four days of her life, Mrs Morrell had been in a continuous coma, as this was demonstrated not to be the case. He had not made any inquiries regarding the symptoms of her stroke and the treatment she had been given for it in the Cheshire hospital where she was first treated. In cross-examining Dr Douthwaite, Mr Lawrence began to exert pressure on this witness: 'It would be most important to know before condemning the doctor's treatment from the outset what actually happened back in Cheshire'. To this, Douthwaite replied: 'It would be interesting to know'.

Lawrence then produced the clinical record

obtained from the hospital in Cheshire, which was another major blow for the prosecution. Lawrence read from the document which covered the ten days in which Mrs Morrell had been at the hospital. This indicated that for every night, there was a record of morphia being injected. Lawrence then asked Dr Douthwaite a pertinent question: 'Does the field of condemnation that you are spreading from this witness-box include Dr Turner of Cheshire for having given the patient morphia after a stroke?' Dr Douthwaite's only response to this was: 'If that was the treatment for the stroke, yes'.

By now, it was becoming very clear that the prosecution's case was collapsing. There had been four doctors who had seen Mrs Morrell, and every one of them had prescribed morphia. This raised the question of whether everyone was wrong, with the exception of Dr Douthwaite, who had never seen her. Quite clearly, he had overstated his case. As the cross examination continued, his absolute certainty became more doubtful when asked by Lawrence what was in the doctor's mind. His guarded reply was: 'I don't know what was in his mind', to which Lawrence retorted: 'Did you not before, when you saw murderous intent?' Douthwaite made no comment. Even the trial judge himself felt that Douthwaite had clearly overstated his case.

The trial lasted a total of sixteen days to become the longest for murder in English criminal history up to that date. By this stage, it had become clear that the case for the Crown was virtually lost. There was no doubt that Dr Douthwaite had been over-persuaded by the prosecution to stick to his original theory regarding the use of opiates. It also served as a reminder to witnesses, that the real strength of any evidence is its reasonableness; it has to be both sound and defensible, and to convince the jury of that fact.

Despite their obvious weak position, the prosecution continued with the Attorney General believing that he could still turn the case around by cross examining Adams himself. He found, to his dismay, that the defence had decided not to call Adams to the witness-stand because Lawrence's 'demolition job' on the prosecution's case had been completely successful.

Defence: Closing Address to the Jury

Geoffrey Lawrence QC began his address to the jury by describing the case before them as being 'one of the most extraordinary'. He then outlined what the Doctor was accused of: 'It is this; that he deliberately murdered an old woman who was his patient at a time when she was already dying and had no more than possibly a very few days or weeks to live'. He then asked the jury to consider: 'Is that not a most extraordinary case that a doctor should be accused of murdering one of his patients when she was dying already'.

With no intervention of the Doctor's part, the end was inevitable, and that was the case alleged against Dr Adams. He then reminded the jury that 'the burden of proof lies on the prosecution and that means that possibility of guilt is not enough, suspicion of guilt is not enough, probability is not enough. It is certainty beyond a reasonable doubt that is required'.

Lawrence then explained to the jury why the accused had not given evidence himself. He outlined the strain under which Dr Adams had laboured during the process of the trial, and that he would be required to recall incidents that happened six years ago. He was unable to refer to any notes and was totally reliant on his own memory-recall. Mr Lawrence then emphasised that any failure on the Doctor's part, however minor, would be interpreted as an indication of guilt, however innocent that failure of recollection or accuracy may be.

Defence counsel then outlined for the jury, the background to the case of Mrs Morrell. Whilst in Cheshire in June 1948, she suffered a stroke. She was described as paralysed, autocratic, difficult and a very wealthy woman. Lawrence then described her first morphine injections given in Cheshire as the most 'significant signpost' in the whole case. The medical prognosis was that she had between six to twelve months to live. The question then arose of what the Doctor could do for her? He could make her life as bearable as possible, give her sleep at night and make her cooperative with the nurses attending her. Dr Adams put her on a course of morphine and heroin, with tablets to ease her pain. What the prosecution was doing, through the evidence of their medical expert Dr Douthwaite, was attacking the Doctor's use of heroin and arousing suspicion regarding its use.

Mr Lawrence reminded the jury that they were not judging whether the Doctor was proficient or not: 'There are good doctors, better doctors, and there are not good doctors, but all are honest men doing their best according to their individual skills'.

He claimed that Dr Adams was doing his duty to the best of his ability by providing his patient with a regular regime of drugs. It had been argued that this was wrong because Mrs Morrell became addicted.

To this view, Mr Lawrence explained that, 'to an old lady with only six to twelve months to live, given to brain problems and outbursts, why should a little dependence on drug therapy matter?'

In September, Adams' partner, Dr Harris, increased morphia because he found the situation worsening, and by November, the patient was dying and the restlessness getting worse. Mr Lawrence asked the question: 'Is a doctor to say, well, you have got very severe pain, and I am therefore entitled to relieve your misery with drugs, or to do nothing?'

Lawrence then put the most crucial question to the jury for their consideration: 'What was in the Doctor's mind when he gave Mrs Morrell these drugs? Was it an intent to kill, or was it an intent to do the best he could with his perhaps rather limited knowledge as a general practitioner, to ease the misery of this dying woman?'

He explained to the jury that on the evening of 12th November, it was clear that the morphia and heroin were not allowing this woman any sleep or peace. Dr Adams' in response to this situation, chose the safest drug available – paraldehyde, a well-established hypnotic drug. He drew the jury's attention to the important point that Dr Douthwaite, the prosecution's medical expert, gave his evidence before the nurses' note-books had been produced.

When asked by the Attorney-General what was his conclusion, he replied: 'I am driven to the conclusion that the Doctor formed the intent to murder on November 8th'. Yet, only two days later, he told the Judge for the first time that he had a theory on the Doctor's withdrawal of morphia on the 1st November.

Lawrence continued: 'On my cross-examination, this theory of the accumulation of morphia in Mrs Morrell's body breaks down. It had been dissented from by two other medical experts, Dr Ashley and Dr Harman. When you have two eminent medical men disagreeing with the whole theory, and if Dr Douthwaite's theory of accumulation in the body is wrong as a scientific fact, then the whole theory of murder comes collapsing to the ground'.

Mr Lawrence then explained to the jury that they were not looking at a morphia death. The doses that were prescribed during the patient's last days were well within the average doses currently prescribed. As the defence expert medical witness, Dr Harman stated: 'People just die'.

Lawrence concluded by stating that, if Mrs Morrell died from natural causes, she did not die as a result of drugs. If she did not die from drugs, then Dr Adams did not kill her, therefore he was not a murderer.

Lawrence then drew the jury's attention to what he considered to be the most significant aspect of the case: 'What I submit is one of the most significant features here, the behaviour of the nurses, trained women. As the case was closed and the last entry made in the note-books, they did not have the slightest suspicion that it wasn't one of the usual unhappy endings to a case, just another case'.

Nearing the conclusion of his closing address to the jury, Lawrence went over the facts of the case for the benefit of the jury. He asked the question of whether it was a murder for gain, because there was no evidence that Dr Adams was, in fact, short of money. He particularly emphasised that the gross value of Mrs Morrell's estate was £175,000. Various people received legacies, but of greater importance was the fact that Dr Adams received just one bequest – some silver in a cupboard valued at £275. The other gift, the pre-war Rolls Royce car was totally dependent upon the son dying before his mother. His comment to the jury was: 'It is too ludicrous to suggest that this doctor embarked upon a course of murder under these circumstances. Yet it is suggested that he had a motive'.

Lawrence then drew the jury's attention to the cremation certificate and particularly to Dr Adams' comment to the police. The doctor could not remember whether or not bequests had come to him or not. Then there was the police evidence when the Doctor is supposed to have told them that he gave nearly all the drugs prescribed to Mrs Morrell. Even if he had in fact stated this, his recollection was certainly incorrect because the records showed that most of the injections were given by the nurses and not by the Doctor.

To emphasise this point, Lawrence stated: 'The point is not what the Doctor prescribed in circumstances which no one could forecast with accuracy, but what was administered, and the evidence for that is in the note-books with Dr Adams' remark: 'Easing the passing of a dying person is not all that wicked, she wanted to die, that can't be murder''.

He further explained that there was a wide difference between giving drugs which shorten life, and giving drugs to ease the passing, not hastening it. Adams' further comment to the police: 'Murder, murder, can you prove it was murder? She was dying anyway' could not be taken as the confession of a guilty man. Lawrence stressed that they were, in fact, the reactions of an innocent man stunned by the mere suggestion of the charge brought against him in his capacity as a doctor.

Lawrence then laid particular emphasis on the fact that 'Trying to ease the last hours of the dying is a doctor's duty, and it has been turned and twisted into an accusation of murder'.

Geoffrey Lawrence concluded: 'Members of

the jury, I do not suppose you will ever forget that for three weeks out of your lives, you were called to sit in judgement. Let it not be a memory that will haunt your conscience. When I have finished, my voice will be silent for the rest of the case. If you think, as I submit, there should be no conviction, be steadfast in that belief to the end, but steadfast and so reach a 'true' verdict'.

Prosecution: Closing Address to the Jury: The Attorney General

The Attorney General opened his address by remarking that the jury would have come to their own conclusions based upon the evidence they had heard and from the documents they had seen proved. He particularly stressed that 'No one wants to see an innocent man convicted on a charge such as this', but that on the evidence he had submitted, they may find it proved that Mrs Morrell was killed by a deliberate act by the Doctor who had killed for profit. He then made a rather contradictory remark that what occurred in the hospital in Cheshire was irrelevant to what took place later. He did agree, however, that since Mrs Morrell had been prescribed morphia whilst in hospital, 'it was not unreasonable to continue for a little while'.

The prosecution's main question for the jury to consider was, why, from July 1948 Dr Adams prescribed morphia in combination with heroin, despite the fact that he had told Superintendent Hannam when he was questioned about the use of these two drugs that 'I very seldom use them'.

A further question was put to the jury: 'Why was she made a drug addict by the Doctor?' The Attorney General volunteered an explanation. In spite of her stroke, Mrs Morrell being given daily heroin injections would enable her to feel some gratitude towards the Doctor, 'a feeling of euphoria' being one of the main characteristics of heroin use. It was further suggested by the prosecution that the Doctor's objective might have been to make: 'This rich lady well-disposed towards him with a view to benefiting under her will'.

A further suggestion was put to the jury in respect to the 'special' injections administered by the Doctor, and the fact that the nurses had no knowledge of their content. It was suggested that this was suspicious. The Attorney-General did acknowledge the fact that there was 'a very significant and important difference between the doses recorded in the nurses' note-books and the prescriptions given by Dr Adams'.

This led to the question of the existence of the note-books themselves, and who had kept them from 1950 to 1957. The nurses had explained that such books were usually destroyed after the patient's death. It was suggested to the jury that there could be only one person who would benefit from their retention – namely Dr Adams. If, as the prosecution had maintained, the Doctor had indeed formed the intent to murder, he would be at pains to secure such vital evidence to avoid incriminating himself.

The Attorney General then turned the jury's attention to the comments made by Dr Adams when informed by the police that he was being charged with the murder of Mrs Morrell: 'Murder? Murder? Can you prove it was murder?'

The prosecuting counsel then offered an alternative explanation to that suggested by Mr Lawrence, the defence counsel: 'Is it, as my learned friend suggested, the incredulous reaction of a man falsely accused? Or is it the sort of statement a shaken man might have made, a man who had committed murder, which he thought could not be proved?'

The jury was then reminded that whilst Dr Adams was on holiday, his partner Dr Harris carried on the course of medication begun by Dr Adams. We are told that Mrs Morrell was very annoyed that Adams had gone on holiday and left her. Why was this? The prosecution suggests that this was, in fact, because Dr Adams had been supplying Mrs Morrell with additional quantities of drugs, unknown to both the nurses attending her, and to Dr Harris. We then hear from the defence how Dr Adams gave instructions for the morphia injections to be stopped.

The prosecution suggested that the stopping of the main sedative, under normal circumstances, indicated that the patient's health was improving rather than deteriorating rapidly. It was this fact that led Dr Douthwaite to conclude that the intention was to terminate the life of Mrs Morrell.

Even the defence's own expert medical witness, Dr Harman, agreed that the policy was to give the patient an injection whenever she woke up, 'to keep her under'. The raised the crucial question of why this was done. The Crown's submission was that there was only one conclusion – 'To hasten death'. Both of the prosecution's medical witnesses, Drs Douthwaite and Ashby agreed that the 'jerky spasms' seen the last night, were due to heroin use. The Attorney General concluded by pointing out to the jury that the defence suggestion that Mrs Morrell died of 'natural causes' was unsustainable. 'On the evidence of the spasms leading up to the day of her death, of the injections of paraldehyde just before her death, to ignore that evidence and to say that her death was due to 'natural causes' would be to ignore the obvious'.

The Attorney General concluded: 'It is my submission, it is proved beyond all reasonable doubt that the cause of the death of Mrs Morrell was the administration of these drugs, and that her death was due to the morphia and the heroin, accelerated by paraldehyde. Members of the jury, murder in this case has been proved. It is for those reasons that I submit to you that the proper verdict in this case is one of murder'.

The Judge's Summing-Up to the Jury: Mr Justice Patrick Devlin

The Judge commenced his summing-up by reminding the jury that they: 'are the sole judges of the fact', and that his task was to interpret the law for them. He told the jury that there were four matters which required explanation, the first of which was the legal definition of murder:

'Murder is an act or a series of acts which were intended to kill and did, in fact, kill.'

The Judge then reminded the jury that there had been a great deal of discussion surrounding the circumstances in which a doctor might be justified in giving drugs which would shorten life in cases of severe pain. Judge Devlin made it abundantly clear that, in law, no special defence was available which covered these circumstances. The Judge then informed the jury of specific instances in which the law made allowance for discretion: 'If the first purpose of medicine – the restoration of health cannot be achieved, there is still much for the doctor to do, and he is entitled to do all that is proper and necessary to relieve pain and suffering, even if the measures he takes, may incidentally shorten life'.

Despite these 'exceptional' circumstances existing, the Judge reinforced the fact that: 'It remains the law, that no doctor has the right to cut off life deliberately'.

The Judge then proceeded to remind the jury of the essence of the case for the defence, which was that the treatment given by Dr Adams was specifically designed to promote comfort and alleviate pain and suffering. If this was considered to be the right and proper treatment, even if it incidentally shortened life, it did not give any grounds for convicting the Doctor of murder. The Judge then drew the jury's attention to the second matter which he regarded as 'one of the most troubling questions in the case'.

Were there any injections administered to Mrs Morrell, over and above those that were recorded in the nurses' note-books? On this specific question, the Judge directed the jury that, as a matter of law, there was no evidence which would lead them to draw such a conclusion.

The jury's attention was then drawn to what the Judge considered to be the third matter of law. This centred on the unavoidable publicity attached to the case, and the fact that the jury must have heard and read a great deal about Dr Adams in the media. In particular, he referred to the press reports covering the preliminary Committal Hearing. The Judge, deviating from normal procedure, expressed his own personal view that the Committal Hearing before the examining magistrates should have been held in private because of prejudicial reporting. He also reminded the jury that those proceedings before the magistrates were significantly different in character to the actual trial procedure. The Judge further warned the jury against paying too much attention to what was in fact, mere suspicions and gossip with no value at all. Instead, they should concentrate on the evidence that really proved something.

The fourth and final matter of law was that the burden of proof was upon the prosecution: 'It is their duty to satisfy you beyond reasonable doubt before you arrive at a verdict of guilty'. The Judge followed this up by stressing to the jury that: 'anything outside the evidence is outside your responsibility. What is not evidence is what you might think the Doctor might have said or not, if he had gone into the witness-box'.

Following on from his last statement, the Judge drew the jury's attention to what he then described as 'an unusual feature, that the accused had not gone into the witness-box'. He then explained that it would be, as a matter of law, 'Utterly wrong if you were to regard the Doctor's silence as contributing in anyway towards proof of guilt'.

This was followed by the Judge drawing the jury's attention to what he considered to be the 'essentials' of the case.

There were three things that had to be proven, and the prosecution had to prove every one of them.

Firstly, it had to prove an act or acts of murder, secondly, to prove that those acts caused the death of Mrs Morrell, and thirdly, that at the time when those acts were committed by the Doctor, he intended to kill. These the Judge regarded as the 'essentials' of the case.

Referring specifically to the 'second' essential, whether the act caused death, the Judge commented on defence counsel's submission. If the act did not cause the death, then the case ends. In respect of this, the defence submitted that the immediate cause of death was not drugs at all. Essentially, it was down to some other 'intervening' cause, possibly another cerebral thrombosis or simply 'old age'.

The Judge then drew the jury's attention to the fact that they had to rely very heavily on the 'medical evidence' to arrive at a satisfactory conclusion, regarding the 'cause' of death.

Dr Douthwaite, the prosecution's expert medical witness's evidence was clear and uncompromising – he regarded the overdose of drugs as the cause of death. The other prosecution witness, Dr Ashby, also regarded this as the 'most likely' cause but, significantly, he could not exclude 'other possibilities'. Dr Harman, the defence's medical expert witness, in contrast, believed that an elderly patient over eighty-years of age, and suffering from cerebral thrombosis: 'may die of anything at any time, and no one can say beyond reasonable doubt, what she actually died of'.

The Judge now turned the jury's attention to what he considered to be the 'central part' of the three 'essential' things, namely the act or acts of murder. He expressed that: 'It is a most curious situation, perhaps unique in these courts, that the act of murder has to be proved by expert evidence'.

What the prosecution were maintaining was that the 'act' was recorded somewhere in the nurses' note-books, but without a doctor to interpret these books, they cannot identify what is thought to be the act of murder. The Judge accepted that: 'It may be that it is much more difficult for the Crown ever to prove that a doctor murders his patient, than it was to prove other acts of murder'.

The prosecution identified three acts which they submitted to the jury, and which the jury had to be satisfied amounted to murder. The first act was the discontinuance of morphia with the specific intent that it should be re-introduced with fatal consequences. This was Dr Douthwaite's theory, but is it too dangerous to adopt this theory? The second act occurred round about 8th November when there occurred a sudden change in the treatment regime for Mrs Morrell for which there was no medical justification. Was this an act which was capable of being a murderous act? The third and final 'act' was Dr Ashby's evidence which did not consider that Mrs Morrell could have survived the sedatives recorded at the doses prescribed.

However, Dr Ashby did agree that there was no maximum dose for opiates, and that Mrs Morrell had not requested an injection at any time. This in effect, blunted the prosecution's insistence that she was 'addicted' to the drugs. He also agreed with defence counsel's suggestion that death could be due to such 'natural' causes as pneumonia or a further stroke.

In view of the 'conflicting' medical opinion, the Judge expressed the view that: 'If you come to the conclusion that Dr Ashby's evidence was 'border-line' evidence, and it does not leave you with a clear impression that this change to 'keeping her under' accelerated death, then you must leave it. In the matter of murder, you can not act upon 'border-line' evidence, therefore you would not be safe in convicting'.

The Judge then advised the jury that if they decide that Mrs Morrell was killed by a course of medically-unjustifiable treatment given her by the Doctor, that they would then have to deal with the question of intent – whether it was done with the intention to murder.

The Judge proceeded to explain to the jury the essentials of 'intention': 'Intention is something that exists in a man's mind. It can only be proved by references that are drawn from his own actions. In considering what was in the Doctor's mind, you must look at the circumstances of the case'.

As regards 'motive', it was assumed from the Attorney General's opening address that the motive in this case was gain. in that the Doctor wished to acquire a legacy by the death of Mrs Morrell. The Judge drew the jury's attention to defence counsel's submission that the chest of silver was a 'pretty paltry reward for murder'.

However, it could not be ignored that the Doctor did display a considerable interest in acquiring some legacy under Mrs Morrell's will. Mr Lawrence for the defence had stated that: 'The suggestion that the Doctor had anticipated her death by a few days or weeks for the sake of a chest of silver worth £270 was ludicrous'. Mr Lawrence also stressed that it was not what the actual position was; whether or not the Doctor was legally entitled to anything, but whether 'he thought he was'.

The only evidence available was the answer the Doctor gave to Superintendent Hannam which makes it quite clear that he knew or thought he knew he was going to inherit the chest of silver and the vintage Rolls Royce car.

The Judge further remarked: 'It must be remembered that it is one thing to give a statement to a police officer, and a quite different thing to go into the witness-box and say it on oath, subject to cross-examination and testing'. It was pointed out that the Attorney General laid particular stress on the statement the Doctor gave to Superintendent Hannam, some of which was difficult to justify on the evidence that was then known. In particular, the phrase that Mrs Morrell was 'in terrible agony' was incorrect because it is now clear that she was not in this situation.

The Judge then commented that the jury might have wished to have heard the Doctor's own explanation of the phrase he used. 'Easing the passing' could have been said innocently but it was, nonetheless, capable of a more sinister connotation. The jury was warned not to take phrases in isolation, but as part of the trend of the Doctor's statements as a whole.

The Judge then expressed the view to the jury

that: 'It seems to me that the statements as a whole do show from the beginning to the end, that it had never crossed his mind that he was faced or might be faced, with the charge of Murdering Mrs Morrell'. At this stage in the proceedings, the Judge indicated that he would sum-up the issues in the case.

There were three points the Crown had to satisfy the jury. Firstly, that Mrs Morrell did not die from natural causes. If it failed to satisfy them of that, they would have to acquit. If it satisfied them, then they go to the second point. The Crown must satisfy them that there emerged an act of killing, something that was capable of being murderous. If that failed, then they were to acquit. If it succeeded, then they would go to the third point. The Crown must satisfy them that if there was an act of that sort, it was done with intent to murder. If that did not satisfy them, they must acquit and if it did satisfy, they must convict.

The Judge speaking to the jury said: 'Mr Lawrence has submitted to you that the whole case against the Doctor from beginning to end is merely suspicion. You sit in judgement to answer one limited question. Has the prosecution satisfied you beyond reasonable doubt that the Doctor murdered Mrs Morrell? On that question, the Doctor stood on his rights and did not speak. I have made it quite clear that I am not criticising that, and I don't criticise it at all. I hope that the day will never come when that right is denied to any Englishman. It is not a refuge of technicality; the law of this matter reflects the national thought of England. So great is our horror at the idea that a man might be questioned, forced to speak and perhaps condemn himself out of his own mouth, that we afford to anyone suspected or accused of a crime at every stage and to the very end, the right to say: 'Ask me no question, I shall answer none. Prove your case'.'

Judge Devlin then gave his concluding comments to the jury: 'This long process ends with the question with which it began. 'Murder? Can you prove it?'' Not infrequently have I heard a case presented by the prosecution that seemed to me to be manifestly a strong one, and sometimes I have felt it my duty to tell the jury so. I do not think, therefore, that I ought to hesitate to tell you that here the case for the defence seems to me to be manifestly a strong one. But it is the same question in the end, always the same; is the case for the Crown strong enough to carry conviction to your mind? It is your question; you have to answer it. It lies always with you, the jury. You will now consider what that answer shall be'.

On the sixteenth day of the trial, the Jury retired to consider their verdict at 11.16 am and at precisely 12 noon they returned to court. The foreman of the jury stood up to answer the Clerk of the Court's question: 'Are you agreed upon your verdict?'

The foreman replied that they were and in response to the question: 'Do you find the prisoner guilty or not guilty?' the reply was 'Not Guilty'.

After the not guilty verdict on the count of murdering Mrs Morrell, the normal process would have been to bring the second indictment regarding Mrs Hullett to trial, either a full trial or, in view of the acquittal in Mrs Morrell's case, so that Adams would plead not guilty, the Attorney-General would offer no evidence, and the judge would direct the jury to bring in a 'not guilty' verdict, which was the course expected by Judge Devlin.

However, the Attorney General, as a minister of the Crown, had the power to suspend an indictment through the legal process of : 'Nolle prosequi' (do not prosecute), something which Judge Devlin said had never been used to prevent an accused from an acquittal, suggesting that this was done because Manningham-Buller did not want a second acquittal, and the loss of both cases that he had indicted. Judge Devlin, writing afterwards in his account of the trial referred to this unusual procedure: 'The use of nolle prosequi to conceal the deficiencies of the prosecution was an abuse of process, leaving an innocent man under the suspicion that there might have been something in the rumours of mass murder after all'.

Manningham-Buller later explained to Parliament after the trial, that the publicity surrounding the Morrell trial would make it difficult to secure a fair trial on the indictment relating to Mrs Hullett, and that this second case depended greatly on inference, which was not supported by admissions as in Mrs Morrell's case. This was a reference to Adam's admissions that he had himself administered most of Mrs Morrell's opiate injections, but in the case of Mrs Hullett he never admitted that he had given more than two barbiturate tablets to Mrs Hullett. The final procedure was that the bail fixed by Eastbourne Magistrates for the offences that Dr Adams faced under the Cremation and Dangerous Drugs Acts had expired during the period of his trial. Mr Lawrence succeeded in obtaining an extension to bail from Judge Devlin. Dr Adams was accordingly discharged, bringing to an end what was regarded as the longest murder trial in English criminal history up to that point in time.

The Post-Trial Period

On 30th June 1957, on his acquittal, John Bodkin Adams resigned from the National Health Service. On 26th July 1957, he appeared at Lewes Assizes before Mrs Justice Pilcher and pleaded guilty to fourteen of the sixteen charges against him. He was fined £150 in respect of eight counts of forging prescriptions, £500 on each of the three counts of making false statements on cremation forms, £250 for the two offences under the Dangerous Drugs Act 1951 and £500 for the one offence of failure to keep a register of drugs as required by the Dangerous Drugs Regulation 1953. The total fines together with additional costs came to £2,400.

Having been convicted of these offences, the judge was obliged to refer the matter to the General Medical Council (GMC). On the 27th November 1957, Adams appeared before the Disciplinary Committee and was struck off the Medical Register as from 30th December 1957. He re-applied to be reinstated to the Register on two occasions, in 1959 and 1960 but failed., before being successful at his third attempt in November 1961.

On this occasion, he informed the GMC that he did not intend to return to general practice but would instead carry out research and continue with consultancy work. Despite all this, Adams still received legacies from his former patients in recognition of his past care for them.

In view of the evidence at Adams' trial, the verdict came as no surprise to the general public, except to the 'sensationally hungry' British press who had been virtually unanimous in their belief of his guilt. One notable exception was *The Daily Express*, who had been convinced of his innocence and who later paid Adams £10,000 to publish his story.

Adam's solicitor announced that he was contemplating proceedings against a number of newspapers. On 26th April 1957, writs were issued against *The Daily Mail*, *The Daily Mirror* and *The News Chronicle*. He later complained to the Press Council regarding a report in *The Daily Herald* on the 4th March 1959. Following this, he issued a libel writ against Associated Newspapers, the publishers of *The Daily Mail*. This case was settled in May 1961, with the defendants apologising and paying damages and costs. As a condition of his settlement, Adams agreed not to proceed against any other newspaper, although it is almost certain that the 'un-named' papers made some contribution towards the cost of the overall settlement.

Adams spent the remainder of his life following his favourite hobby of clay pigeon shooting, serving as President and Honorary Medical Officer of the Clay Pigeon Shooting Association. Whilst out shooting at Battle, Adams broke his leg in a fall on the 1st July 1983, which resulted in him being admitted to Eastbourne General Hospital where he died of heart failure on 4th July 1983. He was cremated and his ashes returned to Coleraine to be buried in the graves of his mother and father.

Chapter Four

An Overview of the Case

The Case in Retrospect

The defendant, John Bodkin Adams, was a doctor who was tried on one count of murdering an elderly patient, Mrs Edith Alice Morrell. The police claimed that Adams had murdered a number of other elderly patients, suggesting that Adams' modus operandi was to administer heroin and morphine with the intention of making his patients addicted and under his influence. By this means, they were induced to leave him legacies in cash and kind in their wills. Finally, he gave them large doses of drugs which caused their deaths. One patient's bequest included a vintage Rolls Royce car although this patient did not, in fact, leave Adams anything in her final will. The police investigated the wills of 132 of Adams' former patients dating from 1946 to 1956, where he had received legacies under those wills. They prepared a list of around 12 names for submission to the prosecuting authorities. On this list were the names of Mrs Morrell, Mrs Gertrude Hullett and two other cases in which evidence had been taken on oath. The Attorney-General chose Mrs Morrell's case, considering it to be the strongest.

This case was based entirely on the police investigation, that Adams either administered or instructed others to administer drugs that killed Mrs Morrell, with the intention of killing her, and that these drugs were unnecessary as she was not suffering pain having been in a semi-comatose state for some time before her death. The prosecution suggested that the motive for Adams deciding to kill Mrs Morrell was because he feared she might alter her will to his disadvantage. Throughout the trial, the prosecution maintained that the motive was a mercenary one. Initially, the prosecution argued that all of the large quantities of morphine and heroin prescribed by Adams in the months prior to Mrs Morrell's death had been injected into her, and that this amount was sufficient to kill her, therefore his only intention was to kill her.

On the second day of the trial, the defence produced the nurses' note-books, which clearly showed that smaller quantities of drugs had been given to the patient than those estimated by the prosecution, these being based on Adams' prescriptions. Significant to the defence case, these note-books recorded that the two injections given the night prior to Mrs Morrell's death, were for paraldehyde, a safe hypnotic drug.

In response to the production of the note-books, one of the prosecution's main medical witnesses changed his testimony from that which he had given Adams' Committal Hearing. Dr Douthwaite had previously introduced a 'new theory' of how Mrs Morrell had been killed. However, this was not accepted by the prosecution's second medical expert, much to the surprise of the prosecution team. This left the prosecution with only one alternative, to argue that the nurses' records were incomplete.

Despite these obvious weaknesses in the prosecution's case, the Attorney General still believed he could turn the case around by cross-examining Adams himself. However, to his complete shock he found that the defence had decided not to call Adams to the witness stand. This in effect, sealed the fate of the prosecution's case against Adams.

The Conduct of the Case

The parties involved in the prosecution case blamed each other for its failure to secure a conviction on the strong belief that Adams should have been convicted. The 'fairness' of this trial has been frequently debated in respect to this supposed failure, particularly with regard to the prejudicial pre-trial press coverage, and the prosecution introducing probably inadmissible evidence at the Committal Hearing. Judge Devlin, the trial judge, thought that Lawrence's concerns that Adams would not receive a fair trial were overstated. However, several legal experts have questioned whether the legal system existing in 1957 would have been capable of giving Adams a fair trial, especially if the 'lost' nurses' notebooks had not come into the hands of the defence.

I believe that the responsibilities of those involved in the initial investigation and final prosecution of Adams' case require some consideration. At the time of the case, the police role was to investigate reports of crimes, determine if one had been committed and arrest a suspect. It was police practice to decide on whether there was a case to prosecute early in their inquiry, then to find evidence to support a prosecution. Then, as today, the role of the Director of Public Prosecutions (DPP) would be to review the case and decide whether a prosecution was appropriate, then appoint counsel to conduct the prosecution. It was also normal practice for the DPP to refer serious crimes to the Attorney General or the Solicitor General. However, for most of the 20th century, the DPP by legal convention, limited consideration of the guilt of the accused based on the evidence collected by the police, in applying what was commonly referred to as the 50% rule, to confirm that there was a 'reasonable chance of conviction', today replaced by 'a reasonable prospect of conviction'. It was not, and still remains, the function of prosecuting counsel to decide guilt or innocence, but to plead their brief.

A valid criticism of the prosecution was that its preparation was weak and poorly presented. The case relied too heavily on the police evidence and the testimony of 'expert' witnesses. Neither of these sources had been thoroughly tested during the pre-trial period. This resulted in the prosecution expressing great concern when the nurses' note-books were produced, literally destroying their case. Finally, the fact that Dr Douthwaite changed his firmly-held opinion, based on what was later considered to be a 'discredited theory. Adding to this, the Attorney General's other counsel, Melford Stevenson's conduct at Adams' Committal Hearing, led to public disclosure of inadmissible evidence that was widely circulated prior to the trial. There is no doubt that Stevenson's unprofessional action was responsible for the sensational and prejudicial media coverage. Finally, there was the Attorney General's failure to adapt his case to the evidence presented by the defence. Instead, he stubbornly proceeded in the hope of relying on Adams' own admissions in cross-examination, which proved fruitless.

The Police Investigation

At a very early stage in the investigation, Hannam firmly believed he had discovered Adams' modus operandi, and that this 'blinkered' his overview of the investigation – a classic example of 'confirmation bias'. As a result of the prosecution's failure to secure a conviction, and criticism of the way in which the police investigation was conducted, the Metropolitan Police conducted an internal investigation into Hannam's conduct during the investigation, in particular his 'close' relationship with the press. Unfortunately, the results of this inquiry were never made public. However, in 1958, Hannam's police career came to an end, and he was later employed in a private security agency.

Suggestions of External Intervention in the Case

In December 1956, the police acquired a memorandum believed to be from a *Daily Mail* journalist concerning rumours of homosexual activity between a police officer, a magistrate and a doctor in Eastbourne (the latter appeared to imply Dr Adams). This information according to the reporter, originated from Superintendent Hannam himself. The 'magistrate' was Sir Roland Gwynne, Mayor of Eastbourne (1929-1931) and brother of Rupert Gwynne, MP for Eastbourne (1910-1924).

Gwynne was Adams' patient and he visited him on a regular basis. They went on frequent holidays together, having spent three weeks in Scotland in the September of 1956. The 'police officer' referred to was Deputy Chief Constable of Eastbourne, Alexander Seekings. What is of special significance in regard to these 'revelations' is that

Superintendent Hannam appears to have ignored these rumours as a possible line of inquiry, despite the fact that homosexual activity was a criminal offence in 1956. This reinforced the belief in Hannam's 'obsession' with the case against Adams. The memorandum clearly revealed the level of Adams' connections with the 'Elite' of Eastbourne at the time. At the same time, there were numerous other rumours circulating that Adams had three 'mistresses', but these were more likely to be just 'cover' stories to avoid too much suspicion. It was true that in 1933, Adams did become engaged to Norah O'Hara, a local butcher's daughter. This was called off two years later because Adams' mother did not approve of him marrying 'below' his status. It has been suggested that Adams, apart for his homosexuality, did not want the fact that he was married to interfere with his well-established relationships with his elderly female patients. However, Adams did remain friends with Norah for the rest of his life, remembering her in his will.

The only recorded instance of intervention in the case concerned the Lord Chief Justice, Lord Goddard. He had proposed to Judge Devlin that in the event that Adams was acquitted in the Morrell case, he should be granted bail before the second charge of murdering Mrs Hullett. This has been regarded by legal observers as a concession to the defence, and as a warning to the prosecution of strong judicial displeasure over the Attorney-General's intention to proceed with the second indictment. Apparently, this was discussed between Judge Devlin and Manningham-Buller after the jury retired to consider their verdict. At the time of the trial, it was believed that the police had overlooked the nurses' note-books which were later 'discovered' by the defence. This differed from the police's own records, in particular, the schedule of exhibits given to the DPP office. This raises the very significant fact that the Attorney-General must have been aware of their existence. This being the case, there must have been high-level 'external' effort to undermine the case against Adams. Not surprisingly, there is no documentary evidence to support this contention, but the usual conspiracy theories abound.

Although the Adams' trial generated a great deal of coverage in the press, it did not feature prominently as being of political significance, in particular due to the Suez crisis at the time. However, George Wigg, the Labour member for Dudley called for an independent inquiry into the conduct of the case on 10th April 1957, but this did not take place, however, the case was debated in Parliament. The major political consequence of the trial was the widespread concerns that the press coverage of the Committal Hearing had prejudiced the subsequent trial.

Ronald Bell, Conservative member for Buckingham South, announced his intention of introducing a private Members' Bill under the ten minute rule to prohibit the reporting of cases during the magistrates hearing. Though this proposal did not materialise, the then Home Secretary established the Tucker Committee to examine the whole question of proceedings before examining magistrates. A report was delivered on the 29th July 1958 with the recommendation that although committal proceedings should continue to be held in public, the reporting of these hearings should be restricted only to the publication of certain 'limited' information, such as the name of the accused and the charges they faced. However, it was nine years before the Home Office finally responded, this culminating in the Criminal Justice Act of 1967.

There were also various concerns expressed regarding the reporting of the case by the foreign press who felt free to print what they liked, whatever the accuracy. In particular the European edition of *Newsweek* published on 1st April 1957, contained certain paragraphs which were regarded as being in contempt of court. Despite the fact that the British were unable to prosecute the American publishers of the magazine, they did however prosecute Eldon Griffiths, *Newsweek*'s European correspondent, together with Rolls House Publishing Company Ltd and WH Smith and Son Ltd for distributing the offending magazine. As a result, Griffiths was acquitted, whilst the two corporate entities were each fined £50 for contempt of court.

Bibliographical Review on the Trial

The first authoritative book to be published on the Adams case was *The Best We Can Do* by Sybille Bedford, the first edition in 1958 being followed by a reprint in 1989. It was Bedford's belief that Adams was innocent of the charge of murder. This was in fact, the only definitive work available that provided a verbatim account of the whole trial. When Adams died in 1983, Rodney Halworth, crime journalist for *The Daily Mail* published *Where There's A Will: The Sensational Life of John Bodkin Adams.* No longer in fear of libel action, Halworth alleged that Adams was a compulsive legacy hunter, that he was guilty of a number of murders, and that the whole prosecution had been mishandled by the Attorney-General. It is clearly apparent that most of the information it contained was from police sources in general and from Herbert Hannam in particular.

The work has been described as 'a sloppy production, careless with detail, presented suspicion as fact, poorly written and unconcerned about its obvious bias'. Following on from this publication, Percy Hoskins published *Two Men Were Acquitted* in 1984. Hoskins was the former crime correspondent of *The Daily Express* and regarded himself as being one of the two men, since Adams's acquittal was also a vindication of his own held belief in Adam's innocence. However, he did take the view that Adams was a 'smug and acquisitive man' who manipulated his patients into re-writing their wills in his favour.

Whilst Adams was not guilty, he was 'naïve' and 'avaricious'. He did however reveal that much of the anti-Adams press coverage had been planted by Scotland Yard to bolster their own investigation and gain credit.

The trial Judge. Patrick Devlin. also wrote his own book on the case entitled, *Easing the Passing* in 1985. This was largely concerned with the various legal and technical issues involved in the trial. Public interest in the case diminished over time but ironically became resurrected in 1999 with the arrest and conviction of Dr Harold Shipman of the murder of fifteen of his patients. As one may expect, this re-awakening of public interest was accompanied by newspaper headlines like: Did Dr Bodkin Adams Murder 400 Patients? in *The Daily Mail* on 31st December 1999. Similarly, 'Copying the model medic who got away with murder' followed in *The Daily Express* on 1st February 2000.

These headlines were based on the notion that Adams had in some way provided the model for Harold Shipman's campaign of murder. These press releases were the inspiration for a new raft of books, the first of which was *The Strange Case of Dr Bodkin*

Adams by John Surtees which appeared in 2000.

Due credit should be given to Surtees in that his book appears to have been 'even-handed', in his treatment of Adam's life, and significantly, it noted that at the time he was practising, it was commonplace for a doctor to receive bequests from their private patients, particularly in situations exactly like those that Dr Adams found himself in. Surtees concluded by regarding Adams as the victim of a 'police vendetta'. What might be called the case for the prosecution came in the form of *A Stranger in Blood: The Story of Dr Bodkin Adams* by Pamela Cullen appearing in 2004. She was the first author to be granted 'official' access to the Scotland Yard case files in 2003 although they were to be closed until 2033. Cullen took the same lines as those by Halworth, the book being marred by the tendency to treat suspicion as fact. However, it was enlivened on this occasion by the introduction of certain conspiracy theories.

The existence of the note regarding the suggestion of a homosexual relationship between a doctor and Roland Gwynne, a previous Mayor of Eastbourne from 1929 to 1931, was taken as 'proof' that Adams was homosexual. Likewise, the fact that Adams attended the 10th Duke of Devonshire during his last days, and that Harold Macmillan was married to the Duke's sister, is also taken as 'evidence' of a strong connection between Adams and the then Conservative government. According to Cullen, Adams may have killed more victims than Shipman. In her view, Adams was acquitted more due to the way the case was presented than to Adams' lack of guilt. She also highlights the fact that Hannam's investigation was 'blinkered' from the perspective of motive.

Opinion of Adams appears to be divided, although in recent years the view has tended towards him being a killer. Sir Patrick Devlin, the trial judge, stated that Adams may have been a 'mercenary killer' but, though compassionate, he was at the same time greedy and prepared to sell death. He did not think of himself as a murderer but a dispenser of death. He could also be convinced that Dr Adams had helped to end Mrs Hullet's life.

All these writers, with the exception of Lord Devlin, based their opinions almost entirely on the evidence given in court regarding the Morrell case. These opinions of Adams portray him as an incompetent doctor lavishly using heroin and morphia, with a successful and lucrative medical practice. However, it should also be realised that between the 1930s and 1960s, the medical profession in general, regarded death as a failure and consequently, subjected dying patients to treatments aimed at prolonging life rather than relieving suffering. This attitude was reflected in the post-war National Health Service, which failed to make adequate provision for end-of-life care. As a result, published medical commentary on care of the dying was very rare before the late 1960s.

The Legal Position of the 'Double Effect' Principle

This principle states that 'an action which has a good objective may be performed despite the fact that the objective can only be achieved at the risk of a harmful effect'. However, this analysis does require some clarification. The action itself must be either good or morally indifferent, the good effect must not be produced by means of the ill-effect, and there must be a proportionate reason for allowing the expected ill effect to occur. It is implicit and vital in this principle that the good effect must outweigh the bad, and this may involve a value judgement. For example, it might well be ethically right to administer pain-killing drugs in such dosage as simultaneously shortens the life of a terminally-ill patient. However, it would not be justified to give the same dose to a young man with identical pain who stood a reasonable chance of recovery.

Judge Patrick Devlin's classic direction was followed in R v Cox (1992) 12. BMLR.38, where the charge to the jury in this case was cited with approval by the House of Lords in Bland, where Lord Goff remarked: 'It is the established rule that a doctor may when caring for a patient who is, for example, dying of cancer, lawfully administer painkilling drugs despite the fact that he knows that an incidental effect of that application, will be to abbreviate the patient's life. Such a decision may properly be made as part of the care of the living patient, in his best interests, and, on this basis, the treatment will be lawful'.
Airedale NHS Trust v Bland, (1993) 1 All ER 821 at 890

There can be no doubt that active euthanasia is unlawful, and this was the position when Dr Nigel Cox was charged in 1991 with the attempted murder of Mrs Lillian Boyes, his patient who was suffering from rheumatoid arthritis, causing her unbelievable pain and suffering. She had expressed a wish to die and was already categorised as 'DNR' (Do Not Resuscitate). Dr Cox injected her with Potassium Chloride, a drug that stops the heart, and has no therapeutic or painkilling properties. Before Dr Cox's action came to the attention of the police, Mrs Boyes was cremated, and it could not be proved 'beyond reasonable doubt' that the injection given by Dr Cox killed her.

Consequently, Dr Cox was convicted only of attempted murder, the judge imposing a suspended sentence, and the General Medical Council (GMC) allowed him to continue in practise, subject to certain conditions. Had the link between his actions and Mrs Boye's death been clearly established, no such course would have been open to the judge. In his summing up to the jury in the Cox case, Judge Ognall stated: 'If a doctor genuinely believes that a certain course is beneficial to his patient, either therapeutically or analgesically, then even though he recognises, that the course carries with it a risk to life, he is fully entitled, nonetheless, to pursue it. If in those circumstances the patient dies, nobody could possible suggest in that situation the doctor was guilty of murder or attempted murder'.

Essentially, the problem for the jury in this case was one of intention. Did Dr Cox intend to kill his patient, or did he hope to give her a short pain-free period during the phrases of dying?

Obviously, we can never know the precise reasons for a jury's verdict, but some factors in the case must have alerted their attention. Mrs Boyes was incurably but not terminally ill, and Dr Cox injected a non-therapeutic substance. It is reasonable to assume that while public opinion in the United Kingdom will give great latitude to the medical profession in its fight against suffering, it is not yet prepared to accept the use of a substance with no analgesic effect, and which is known to be lethal when injected in concentrated form. As a result of this, Dr Cox was unable to plead 'double effect' or even the defence of 'necessity'.

The law condemns active euthanasia on the

ground of intent. The terminally ill are beyond curative therapy by definition, and, therefore, their management becomes a matter of the relief from pain and suffering. Achieving this may, inevitably, involve some risk to life but it is the patient's comfort not their premature death, which should be the intended outcome. However, it is the terminally ill patient who most significantly sets the scene for the application of the concept of 'double effect'.

In 1957, at a meeting of the British Medical Association, the use of heroin to induce euphoria and oblivion was advocated. Although doctors were aware that hastening a patient's death was illegal, it was suggested that it was something that 'the law forbids in theory but ignores in practice'. In Adams' case, the court did not ignore the suggestion that he had hastened death and , as Judge Devlin made clear, he needed to clarify for the jury, and incidentally for the medical profession, the extent to which the law allowed the orthodox doctor to go in 'easing the passing' of the dying. Mahar regards Adams' statements to Hannam on Mrs Morrell as less about his guilt or innocence than a disconnection between the medical and legal views on assisted dying. Adams never denied giving his patients large doses of opiates, but denied it was murder.

This was not simply Adams' idiosyncratic view, as appears from the evidence of Dr Douthwaite for the prosecution, who accepted that a physician might knowingly give fatal doses of pain relieving drugs to a terminally ill patient. Devlin's directions to the jury confirmed that it was a 'medical' issue not a legal one, whether Adams' treatment was designed to promote comfort for Mrs Morrell. Devlin's view was that Adams may have been guilty of mercy-killing, but he was one who cared for his patients to the best of his ability. Adams eased the passing of Mrs Morrell, but his greed brought his motives into question. Mahar notes an editorial in a medical journal following the case, which suggested that the publicity it caused might hamper medical discretion but claimed the use of opiates in terminal cases was essential. Adams may be seen as an extreme case in their use, yet other doctors also used them.

Psychological Profile of Adams

Dr Richard Badcock, the consultant psychiatrist who interviewed Harold Shipman, compared the characteristics of Shipman with those of Adams. The main differences between the two was that Shipman injected morphine intravenously usually killing the patient within minutes. In contrast, Adams preferred to sedate his victims, sometimes over lengthy periods of weeks or even months before their eventual death. However, one common thread was that they both preferred to work alone, rather than in group practice. Also, they both appear to have worked extended hours, often turning up unannounced at their patients' homes. Both had reputations for being rude, egotistic and uncompromising. The most significant characteristic was that they both paid many visits to patients who were not, as far as their medical records showed, ill or in need of medical attention.

Shipman's most overt characteristic was his display of self-importance, attention-seeking and a super-inflated ego. In contrast, Adams' arrogance was more muted and masked by his ingratiating expressions and overt religiosity. According to Badcock, they were both 'straight-forward psychopaths'.

There is evidence in Adams' activities and

life-style that clearly indicate a sense of entitlement, yet he felt empty, living his life on the fringes. He did appear obsessed with the lives of the affluent and desperately wanted their lifestyle for himself. The closest Adams came to sustaining a relationship was with his mother who was possessive, domineering and highly critical. Here we can identify parallels with Shipman and his mother who died whilst he was a teenager. As a remedy for all his missed opportunities, Adams in company with Shipman, liked the feeling of control he had over his patients. Many believe him to have been a serial killer on a large scale. However, unlike Shipman, there are no obvious patterns which, taken together, confirm this assertion, only lingering 'suspicious circumstances'.

It has been further suggested that Adam's over-pious religious behaviour replaced a morality in which he viewed himself as a 'saviour' killer. Adams experienced severe personal loss during his formative teenage years with the death of his father and brother. It is believed that he had an over-dependent relationship with his mother. His one attempt to escape the impasse, was his engagement to Norah O'Hara which his mother wrecked. By the time his mother died, it was too late to rekindle this relationship. As regards Adams' alleged homosexuality, this must have influenced his view of himself as being on the periphery of society and leading a 'double life'.

There were also social factors influencing Adams' personal behaviour, coming as he did from a humble, pious family background in Ireland.

This goes some way to explaining his craving for recognition within the upper echelons of Eastbourne's society. This also influenced his perception of class distinction and social divisions so prominent in Eastbourne, as in other towns, with the belief that there were 'double standards', with one set of rules for the 'establishment', and one for others.

John Bodkin Adams undoubtedly killed many of his patients, and he admitted so himself, although from his point of view, he was simply 'easing the passing' of his dying patients. As far as the medical profession was concerned at the time, there was nothing particularly unusual in this practice.

In 1936, George V was helped by his royal physician, Bertrand Edward Dawson, who injected the king with morphine and cocaine to 'help him on his way'. No prosecution was ever brought against Dr Dawson for this clear act of euthanasia. Scotland Yard's files on the Adams case and those of the Director of Public Prosecutions were to be closed to public scrutiny until 2033.

However, these files were opened to public scrutiny in 2003. The following extracts reveal those witness statements gathered by Superintendent Hannam during the investigation, which supported his suspicions as regards Adams' activities. These statements were never revealed during the trial.

'August 1939 – Adams was treating Mrs Agnes Pike when her solicitors became concerned about the amount of opiate drugs she was being prescribed by Adams and requested another doctor, Dr Matthew to take over from Adams. He examined the patient in the presence of Adams and could find no disease present. According to Dr Matthew, 'the patient was deeply under the influence of drugs incoherent and visibly confused'. Later during the examination, Adams administered an injection of morphia, the purpose according to Adams was because 'she might become violent'. Dr Matthew also discovered that Adams had banned all the patient's relatives from seeing her. Once Dr Matthew took over the care of this patient, he withdrew Adam's medication and within eight weeks under his care, Ms Pike regained her full faculties.'

'December 24 1946 – Emily Louise Mortimer died, aged 75. Following her death, Adams took a bottle of brandy and a clock from her room. He claimed to the police that the clock had been loaned to Ms Mortimer by him and that it was not 'right to leave spirits in a nursing home'. Adams received the residue from Mortimer's will and by 1957 had earned £1,950 in dividends from the shares he inherited.'

'23 February 1950 – Amy Ware died, aged 76. Adams had banned her from seeing her relatives prior to her death. She left Adams £1,000 of her total estate of £8,993, yet Adams stated on the cremation form that he was not a beneficiary of the will. He was charged and convicted of this in 1957.'

'December 1950 – Annabelle Kilgour died, aged 89. She had been attended by Adams since July when she had a stroke. She went into a coma on 23 December, immediately after Adams started giving her sedatives. The nurse involved in her care later told the police she was 'quite certain Adams either gave her the wrong injection or far too concentrated a type'. Kilgour left Adams £200 and a clock.'

'3 January 1952 – Adams purchased 5,000 phenobarbitone tablets and by the time his house was searched prior to his arrest four years later, none were found.'

'11 May 1952 – Julia Bradnum died, aged 85. The previous year Adams asked her if her will was in order and offered to accompany her to the bank to check it. On examining it, Adams pointed out that she had not given her beneficiaries 'addresses' and that it should be re-written. She had wanted to leave her house to her adopted daughter, but Adams suggested it would be best to sell the house and then give money to whoever she wished. This she did, Adams received £661. The day before Bradnum died, she had been doing housework and going for walks. The next morning she woke up feeling unwell. Adams was called and saw her. He gave her an injection and stated 'It will be over in three minutes'. It definitely was, and Adams confirmed 'I'm afraid she's gone' and left the room. Bradnum's body was exhumed on 21 December 1956. Adams had stated on the death certificate that her cause of death was 'cerebral haemorrhage'. The forensic pathologist Dr Francis Camps examined her brain and excluded this possibility. The rest of the body was not in a state to deduce the real cause of death. It was also noticed that Adams her executor, had put a plate on Bradnum's coffin stating she died on 27 May 1952, yet this was the date her body was interred.'

22 November 1952 – Julia Thomas aged 72, was being treated by Adams for depression after her cat died in early November. On the 19th, Adams gave sedatives so she would feel 'better for it in the morning'. The next day, after more tablets, she went into a coma. On the 21st Adams told Thomas's cook that 'Mrs Thomas promised him her typewriter, I'll take it now'. She died at 3 am the next morning.

15 January 1953 - Hilda Neil Miller, aged 86, died in

a guest house where she lived with her sister Clara. One of Hilda's friends asked Adams if he would visit Hilda which he did. Adams was seen by Hilda's nurse to pick up articles in her room and then slip them into his pocket. Adams arranged Hilda's funeral and burial.

22 February 1954 - Clara Neil Miller died aged 87. Adams often locked the door of her room when he saw her for up to twenty minutes at a time. When one of her friends asked about this curious practice, Clara said he was assisting her in 'personal matters' such as pinning on brooches, adjusting her dress. She also appeared to be under the influence of drugs. Clara left Adams £1,275, and he charged her estate a further £700 after her death. He was the sole executor of her will. Her funeral was arranged by Adams and only he and Anne Sharp, the guest house owner were present. She received £200 in Clara's will. Clara's was one of the two bodies exhumed during the police investigation on 21 December 1956. Francis Camps concluded that she had broncho-pneumonia possibly brought about by high drug doses, but not a heart problem as Adams had stated on her death certificate. According to prescription records, Adams had not prescribed anything to treat the broncho-pneumonia.

30 May 1955 – James Downs, brother-in-law to Amy Ware, died, aged 88. He had become a resident at a nursing home as a result of a broken ankle. Adams treated him with a sedative containing morphia, which made him very forgetful. On 7 April Adams gave his nurse a tablet to make him more alert. Two hours later, a solicitor arrived for him to amend his will. Adams informed the solicitor that he was to be made a legatee to inherit £1,000. The solicitor

amended the will and returned two hours later accompanied by another doctor, Dr Barkworth, who declared the patient to be alert. The doctor was paid 3 guineas for his time. Down's nurse, Miller informed the police later that she had overheard Adams in April telling Downs that he hadn't mentioned Adams in his will. Downs died after suffering a coma which lasted 36 hours, only 12 hours after Adams' last visit. Adams charged his estate £216 for his services to Downs and also signed his cremation form, stating he had 'no pecuniary interest in the death of the deceased.'

14 March 1956 - Alfred John Hullett died, aged 71, the husband of Gertrude Hullett. Shortly after his death, Adams collected a prescription from a chemist in Eastbourne for a 10cc hypodermic solution containing 5 grains of morphine, made out in the name of Mr Hullett, the prescription to be back-dated to the previous day. The police presumed this was to cover morphine Adams had given him from his own personal supply. Mr Hullett left Adams £500 in his will.

15 November 1956 – Annie Sharpe, owner of the guest house where the Millers died and considered to be a major witness, died suddenly of cancer. Adams had diagnosed this five days earlier and made a prescription for her to receive injections of morphine and tablets of pethidine. She was cremated hastily. During his investigations, Superintendent Hannam had discovered that four members of Adams' own household had been prescribed either morphine, heroin or pethidine by Adams, all obtained on the NHS. This led Hannam to conclude that he was using their names and keeping the drugs for his own private

supply, a certain act of fraud.
Source: John Bodkin Adams Wikipedia page.

Following Adams' death, there were comments circulating both locally and nationally, which, on the whole, were supportive of Adams. There were firmly-held views that Superintendent Hannam had encouraged press and local gossip by his suggestion that Adams was a 'mass murderer'. This could only have been for his own personal gratification.

Lord Devlin, in his detailed account of the trial, expressed that: 'The public is swept by waves of emotion which it doesn't reason about. No one wanted to hear about the possible innocence of Dr Adams, long before he was tried. He may well have blurred the distinction between helping symptoms and helping to die'.

The fact was that having Scotland Yard investigating the rumours surrounding Adams' activities lent support to innuendo and rumours. Professor Keith Simpson, the distinguished forensic pathologist remarked in his account of the trial that 'It is lawful to ease the process of dying. That is not euthanasia but a humane service. Drugs which can help can also kill, and there is no sharp definition between painless sleep and death'.

The Legal Issue of 'Causation'

The criminal law does not seek to punish people for their evil thoughts, but for their conduct. Where charged with a crime, the prosecution must prove the accused's acts or omissions caused the outcome. There are two strands to causation; factual and legal. Factual causation is where it must be proved that the outcome would have occurred but for the conduct of the accused. Legal causation is related to ideas of responsibility and culpability. On questions of legal causation, the jury will be directed to consider whether the accused's act was more than minimal in contributing towards the victim's death.

Here in Adams' case. a doctor faced a murder charge for providing his patient with pain-relieving drugs which led to an acceleration of the patient's death. The jury were directed by Devlin J, to consider that no act constituted murder unless it caused death. By 'cause' Devlin J, explained that it was not a scientific, technical or philosophical definition but what the jury would consider to be 'common sense'. Presumably, a jury's moral reaction would be that the doctor's sole aim was to relieve pain and that it was 'incidental' that the patient's death was accelerated. However, had it been a sole beneficiary who injected the patient with the aim of accelerating the patient's death so that they could benefit from their inheritance, then the jury's moral reaction was likely to be that the beneficiary caused the death. It does appear in R v Adams that the issue of causality became mixed up with the issue of motive because there was a strong moral imperative to clear the doctor of liability.

This led to the causality of the doctor's actions being doubted rather than his mental state (mens rea) of the offence. It was thought that a special defence was created to distinguish the doctor from a murderer in cases of life-shortening palliative care. It has been argued by some that Dr Adams was no different to Dr Harold Shipman who was also acting outside the law. The moral judgement of the judiciary can and clearly has, affected the application of the legal rules in relation to criminal causation. In R v Adams, this is a classic example where the law is clear that the doctor should have been guilty, as his actions caused the patient's death. However, in this case, there was a divergence of views between the medical profession and certain members of the police.

The debate about whether or not Adams was a murderer comes down to an argument about medical ethics and the question of euthanasia. There were certainly those that believed Adams to be a killer. The barrister Melford Stevenson (who led the prosecution at Adam's Committal Hearing) was of the opinion that he was 'incredibly lucky to have literally got away with murder'. The Scotland Yard Detective, Sergeant Charles Hewitt, whose views appeared in *The Times* of 11th July 1983, claimed that Adams was 'without doubt a mass murderer who deserved to be hanged 20 times over'.

However, the trial judge, Patrick Devlin, wrote: 'I certainly don't believe that he was a mass murderer' but instead described him as 'a mercenary killer'. There are, however, those who claim that Adams was essentially 'the victim of a vicious whispering campaign of rumour and vilification' as to how many he might have or have not killed, and claims that he killed 400 people are entirely fanciful, relating back to 'unsubstantiated and sensational' newspaper headlines.

Though a defendant had never been required to give evidence in their own defence, Judge Devlin reinforced in his summing-up that no prejudice should be attached by the jury to the fact that Adams did not give evidence.

The forensic pathologist Francis Camps believed that there were 163 'suspicious' cases. However, much of the 'solid evidence' for these assertions turned out to be false. It is likely that the nurses who perjured themselves at the trial had no real intention of doing so. Having been asked to recall the details of the treatment of a patient who had died almost six years previously, no doubt the nurses tried to be as helpful as possible to the police, and unintentionally told them what they wanted to know.

There was no doubt within legal circles, that Mannigham-Buller did aspire to the office of Lord Chief Justice but his 'lack-lustre' performance in the Adams case counted against him. However, whether the prosecution would have been more successful with a charge of manslaughter, given the divergence of the crucial expert medical opinion, is anyone's guess.

There is also suspicion that the police themselves wanted their share of the 'kudos and glory' of prosecuting a doctor for murder. Ironically, they had to wait another forty years before Harold Shipman became the first to be successfully prosecuted for homicide.

Few names strike fear and disgust in equal measure to the hearts and minds of the British general public as does Dr Harold Shipman, the general practitioner who was convicted in 2000 of murdering 15 of his patients.

Going back 50 years and we have a similar case with the trial of Dr John Bodkin Adams, the only difference here being that he was acquitted. However, there are remarkable similarities in the psychological profile of both of these people.

    Bodkin Adams had an empty life and a sense of entitlement leading to his desire for social acceptance. It is believed that he killed not out of greed for money but instead, to cope with his resentment and social exclusion. Similarly, Shipman wasn't motivated by money, but by death itself, gaining satisfaction and pleasure from killings his patients.

    Prior to Dr Harold Shipman's conviction, and 25 years after the Adams case, another British doctor, Leonard Arthur, stood trial for murder arising from medical treatment. Arthur was tried in November 1981 at Leicester Crown Court for the attempted murder of John Pearson, a newborn child with Down's syndrome. Similar to Adam's case, on the advice of his legal team, Arthur did not give evidence in his defence, relying instead on expert medical witnesses. He was subsequently acquitted. In 2000, Harold Shipman became the only British doctor to be successfully prosecuted for the murder of his patients. He was found unanimously guilty on 15 counts and the Shipman Inquiry concluded in 2002 that he had murdered another 200.

    In conclusion, the vital question still remains: was John Bodkin Adams the mass murderer many believed him to be, or was he in fact, the bringer of comfort and peace to the dying?

    Dear Reader, the verdict is yours!

Appendices

Appendix A
Memorandum from the Attorney General

The Current Law of Homicide

Murder

'Murder is defined as 'unlawful killing with malice aforethought'. This is to be contrasted with those forms of manslaughter which consist of killing without 'malice aforethought'.

The principal distinguishing feature between murder and manslaughter is that murder requires an intention to kill or to cause grievous bodily harm.

The penalty for murder is life imprisonment.

In summary, deliberately taking the life of another person, whether the person is dying or not, constitutes the crime of murder. Accordingly, any doctor who practices mercy killing can be charged with murder if the facts are clearly established.

The only exception is where the doctor acts to do all that is proper and necessary to relieve pain with the incidental effect that this will shorten the patient's life.

This was explained by Devlin J. in R v Adams [1957] Crim L.R. 773. Doctor Adams was charged with the murder of a patient. It was alleged that he had prescribed and administered large quantities of drugs that he must have known that death would result. In his summing up to the jury, Devlin J. stated: 'If her life was cut short by weeks or months it was just as much murder as if it was cut short by years. There has been much discussion as to when doctors might be justified in administering drugs which would shorten life. Cases of severe pain were suggested and also cases of helpless misery. The law knows no special defence in this category.'

However, he went on to say: '...but that does not mean that a doctor who was aiding the sick and dying had to calculate in minutes, or even hours, perhaps, not in days or weeks, the effect on a patient's life of the medicines which he could administer. If the first purpose of medicine – the restoration of health – could no longer be achieved there was still much for the doctor to do and he was entitled to do all that was proper and necessary to relieve pain and suffering even if the measures he took might incidentally shorten life by hours or perhaps even longer'.

This introduced into English law the 'double-effect' principle, that is if an act has two consequences, one good and one bad, the bad consequence may nevertheless be acceptable depending on the circumstances.

Source: House of Lords – Assisted Dying for the Terminally Ill Bill - Minutes
(Parliamentary Copyright 2005)

Appendix B

'All I Tried To Do Was Relieve His Agony, His Distress And Suffering'

'Campaigners for the legalisation of euthanasia were jubilant last night after a jury unanimously found a family doctor who gave an elderly patient a massive overdose of diamorphine not guilty of murder after only 69 minutes' deliberation. The case has ignited a nationwide debate about the rights and wrongs of hastening the deaths of terminally ill patients. The Voluntary Euthanasia Society called the acquittal of GP David Moor at Newcastle-upon-Tyne Crown Court a 'huge relief' to doctors and patients throughout Britain, but said guidelines were urgently needed to tell doctors how they could help dying patients without risking a similar prosecution. Had Dr Moor of Stamfordham, Northumberland, been convicted of murdering 85-year-old George Liddell, a cancer sufferer, he would have faced a life sentence, which is mandatory for murder.

Peggy Norris, chairwoman of the anti-euthanasia group Alert, said: 'I think this is a sad day for medicine as it makes the law unclear as to what is allowed. We cannot have a half-law when it comes to this'. The government is firmly opposed to legalising euthanasia, but the case is likely to spark renewed calls for the abolition of the mandatory life sentence for murder, a move favoured by senior judges. Dr Moor, 52, a high-profile GP who retired early because of the stress of the case, thanked all those who supported him through his 'extraordinary ordeal'. He specifically thanked Mr Lidell's son-in-law, Tony Ryan, who told the court he was a 'wonderful doctor'. The GP added: 'In caring for a terminally ill patient, a doctor is entitled to give pain relieving medication which may have the effect of a patient's death. All I tried to do in treating Mr Liddell was to relieve his agony, distress and suffering. This has always been my approach in treating my patients with care and compassion. Doctors who treat dying patients to relieve their pain walk a tightrope to achieve it'.

Dr Moor, who practised in Newcastle upon Tyne, was the first British doctor to be tried for murder purely for the mercy killing of a patient. In the only other murder case that of John Bodkin Adams in 1957, the Crown alleged that the doctor profited from the death of an elderly widow. He was acquitted. Dr Moor, a popular GP who broadcast on regional radio and wrote for a local newspaper, was arrested after a press interview in which he claimed to have helped many patients to 'pain -free' deaths. He denied in court that he had ever murdered anybody. His defence rested on the principle of 'double effect', which lays down that doctors may legally administer drugs which hasten a patient's death, as long as the intention was to ease suffering. The prosecution alleged that the huge dose of diamorphine, three times higher than Dr Moor had admitted administering, must have been intended to kill Mr Liddell, a retired ambulance man.

The jury delivered its verdict after a summing up by Mr Justice Holland which nudged them towards an acquittal. He told them they might consider it ironic that Dr Moor found himself facing the charge because he was caring enough to come out on his day off to see Mr Liddell. The turning point in the case came when the judge excluded key toxicological evidence, leaving the prosecution with no proof that the injection had caused the death. The judge awarded the defence team only two-thirds of the costs, saying

Dr Moor had partly brought the prosecution on himself by 'very silly remarks to the press' and lying to the NHS and police'. The Crown Prosecution Service defended its decision to prosecute. A spokesman said: 'Advice was obtained from senior treasury counsel, a member of the independent bar, and it was decided that a prosecution was required'. Michael Wilks, chairman of the British Medical Association's medical ethics committee said, 'The trial should not be seen as breaking new ground on the issue of euthanasia'.
Source: *The Guardian*, 12th May 1999, by Clare Dyer, Legal Correspondent.

Selected Bibliography

BEDFORD, S, *The Best We Can Do*, Penguin, London (1989).

CULLEN, P, *A Stranger in Blood: The Case Files on Dr John Bodkin Adams*, London, Elliott and Thompson (2006).

DEVLIN, P, *Easing the Passing: The Trial of Doctor John Bodkin Adams*, London, The Bodley Head, (1985).

HALLWORTH, & WILLIAMS, M, *Where There's a Will: The Sensational Life of Dr John Bodkin Adams*, Jersey, Capstan Press, (1983).

HOSKINS, P, *Two Men Were Acquitted: The Trial and Acquittal of Doctor John Bodkin Adams*, London, Secker and Warburg, (1984).

MAHAR, C, *Easing the Passing: R v Adams and Terminal Care in Post-War Britain, Social History of Medicine, Vol 28, No 1* (2012).

OTLOWSKI, M, *Voluntary Euthanasia and the Common Law*, Oxford UP (2004).

ROBINS, J, *The Curious Habits of Dr Adams: A 1950s Murder Mystery*, London, John Murray, (2013).

SIMPSON, AWB, 'The Trial of Dr John Bodkin Adams' in the *Michigan Law Review*, vol 84, No 4/5 (1986).

SURTEES, J, *The Strange Case of Dr Bodkin Adams: The Life and Murder Trial of Eastbourne's Infamous Doctor, and the views of those who knew him*, Eastbourne, (2000).

Lightning Source UK Ltd.
Milton Keynes UK
UKHW021316220822
407649UK00010B/2287